Robert G Kissick

The Irish Prince and the Hebrew Prophet

Robert G Kissick

The Irish Prince and the Hebrew Prophet

ISBN/EAN: 9783741187087

Manufactured in Europe, USA, Canada, Australia, Japa

Cover: Foto ©Lupo / pixelio.de

Manufactured and distributed by brebook publishing software
(www.brebook.com)

Robert G Kissick

The Irish Prince and the Hebrew Prophet

THE IRISH PRINCE

AND

THE HEBREW PROPHET

A Masonic Tale of the captive Jews and
the Ark of the Covenant

By the author of
"THE JERICO PAPERS"

LIA FAIL

"Unless the fates have faithless grown,
And prophet's voice be vain,
Where'er is found the sacred stone
The wanderer's race shall reign."—CELTIC BARD
Translated by Sir WALTER SCOTT

NEW YORK
MASONIC PUBLISHING COMPANY
NO. 63 BLEECKER STREET
1896.

PRESS OF
EDWARD O. JENKINS' SON,
NEW YORK.

TO

Mrs. HENRY WARD BEECHER

THE AGED AND BELOVED FRIEND OF MY FAMILY

This Book

IS AFFECTIONATELY DEDICATED

CONTENTS.

CONTENTS.

PREFACE.

On Tuesday, Dec. 20, 1881, the Rev. George W. Greenwood was ordained pastor of the First Identity Church of Brooklyn, N. Y. The council was composed of the Rev. Edward Beecher, D.D., Rev. J. F. Halsey, D.D., Rev. William James and the Rev. George Nixon. The founding of the church was in order to prove the identity existing between the Lost Tribes of the Children of Israel and the Anglo-Saxon race. The identification is completed when we compare the pages of the " Heir of the World," edited by George W. Greenwood, and the " Forty-seven Identifications of the Anglo-Saxons with the Lost Ten Tribes of Israel," by Edward Hine, with Holy Writ.

When Jacob blessed Joseph's children, he created by that act the Thirteenth Tribe, making Ephraim many mighty nations and Manasseh a great people. The term Ephraim is synonymous with Joseph ; that is, we speak of them as one, from the fact that Ephraim inherited the birthright, while Manasseh, the Thirteenth Tribe, was destined to become a great people. If we examine Revelations we shall find that at the time of the sealing of the Twelve Tribes of the Children of

Israel Dan is cast out, and in the place of Dan is Manasseh.

Thus you see that the blessing by Jacob was an inspiration of Divine Providence, for there must be twelve tribes, and if Dan was to be cast out, then there must be a thirteenth tribe to make the twelve good. Just the same as in the case of the twelve disciples. Judas Iscariot was cast out, and Matthias, or the thirteenth disciple, was appointed to fill his place. Having made clear the relative position of the two lads, let us compare the Scriptures with accepted history and see how far the prophecies have been fulfilled. First, they were to be a multitudinous people; strong in power; speaking another tongue; an island nation having large colonies; a monarchy, and a Christian people. This is Ephraim.

Now, whenever we find Manasseh, we must find them according to Scripture, "a great people," having come out and separated themselves from the house of Ephraim, bearing the same name and identity, speaking the same language, bearing the same cross, and proclaiming the same Christianity. "The children that thou shalt have, after thou hast lost the other," says Isaiah. What other? Why, the house of Manasseh, or "the great people," for these, under divine blessing, were all she could ever lose, and although few in number at the time of separation, could never be conquered.

Ephraim's, or England's peculiar characteristic, even unto this day, is in pronouncing the letter H, consequently the first war between Ephraim and Manasseh, "the great people," resulted disastrously for Ephraim, as it did in all her future battles with that nation, which is known not only as Manasseh, but Gilead. The Ephraimites sent a spy into the camp of Gilead, but he was immediately detected, "for they say unto him, 'Say now Shibboleth,' and he said 'Sibboleth,' for he could not frame to pronounce it right." "Then they took him and slew him at the passage of Jordan, and there fell at that time of the Ephraimites forty and two thousand." Thus Ephraim, "the many mighty nations," has never been able to overcome Manasseh, "the great people." Some few weeks ago, an Englishman, fresh from London, came into my office, and during the course of conversation said he had friends living in Art and Alsey streets, meaning Hart and Halsey. Thus he spoke, because he could not frame to pronounce the H.

The blessings that followed these two great nations were: First, they should be a pushing people. "His glory is like the firstlings of his bullock." (This is why we call England John Bull.) "His horns like the horns of the Unicorn, with them they shall push the people to the ends of the earth," and they are "the thousands of Manasseh, and the ten thousands of Ephraim." You will notice that the horns of the Unicorn were given to the two lads.

Now it is a singular fact that after the Pilgrims settled down in Massachusetts, Oliver Cromwell knocked
off one of the horns of the British Unicorn, and since
that time it has been represented with only one horn.
A great many people, in reading the Scriptures, when
they see the house of Israel mentioned, think they are
the Jews, and also that Israel means the Church, yet
nowhere in the Bible is Israel mentioned as the Church,
but always as a nation. Paul says, "When I am with
the Jews, I am as a Jew, and when I am with the
Greeks, I am as a Greek, but I am neither; I am an
Israelite of the tribe of Benjamin." How easily Peter
was recognized as a Galilean. "Thou art a Galilean,"
said the maid, "and thy speech betrayeth thee."

So you see the Israelites kept themselves separated
from the Jews, even in the days of Christ, and this passage of Scripture will throw great light upon it, viz.:
"Now Jesus walked no more openly with the Jews, but
went away to a city called Ephraim, and dwelt with
His disciples." Having shown you the difference between the Israelites and the Jews, let us see what difference there is in the prophecies concerning them.

The house of Judah is composed of two tribes,
viz.: Judah and Levi, and they are the Jews of the
present day, having never lost their name nor their
identity, and who are to-day living under the Law of
Moses, and the curse of their own prayer. Jeremiah
says of them that they should always retain their

name and identity, under the Mosaic law, without a government, and strangers tolerated in all foreign countries.

How different the prophecies concerning Israel. Unknown in name, a multitudinous people, strong in power, speaking another tongue, many mighty nations, and a Christian people. Seven hundred and twenty-five years B.C. the house of Israel went into the Assyrian captivity, from which they have never returned. Six hundred and six years B.C. the house of Judah went into the Babylonian captivity, and were held seventy years, after which they were liberated by Cyrus and became a dependency up to the year seventy A.D., when Titus besieged Jerusalem. They were then overthrown and scattered to the four winds of heaven, even unto this day.

The tribe of Benjamin separated themselves from the house of Israel and united with the house of Judah, and we find the design of this union in First Kings. Judah was to reject Christ, yet he had chosen the city of Jerusalem, and this city was in Benjamin's territory, and contained the temple as well as the throne of David, which was to have an heir until Shiloh came, and as Judah refused, Benjamin was selected, as all of the disciples were Benjaminites, save Judas Iscariot.

In the year 70, when Titus besieged Jerusalem, the Christians made their escape, and ancient writers say they were all of the tribe of Benjamin. The walls were ordered to be battered down, after which the army retired to rest, and during this time the Benjaminites all made their escape, and when Titus called his commanding general to an account he was speechless. In this we find the prophecy of Jeremiah literally fulfilled, when he says: " Oh, ye children of Benjamin, gather yourselves together and flee out of the midst of Jerusalem, for evil appeareth out of the north," and in fulfillment of this very prophecy the Benjaminites escaped and afterward entered England.

The tribe of Dan were a seafaring people, owning from Joppa, fifty miles south, on the coast of the Mediterranean Sea, and controlling nearly all the shipping since the days of David ; consequently a large number of them had immigrated to Ireland, and were known as Danites.

David's sceptre had ruled over Israel up to the time of the Babylonish captivity, when Zedekiah had his eyes put out, and his sons killed before him, but he had two daughters, the beautiful princess, Tea Tephi, and Myra, who remained in Jerusalem, and were saved alive. When Jeremiah and Baruch were released from the dungeon by order of Nebuchadnezzar they found them, and also secured the ark of the covenant, the tables of the law which were in the ark, and Jacob's Pillar, and boarding one of Dan's ships went to the province of Ulster, in Ireland ; and here ancient Irish history comes majestically to our relief, for it is an indisputable historical fact that in 580 B.C. there arrived in the North of Ireland a Hebrew princess whose name was Tea Tephi, and she was accompanied by two men, one of whom was a prophet.

From this time a new era was enacted under the tribe of Dan, who are the Danites. The name of the city was changed from Lothair Crofin to Tara, a Hebrew word, signifying the law of the two tables; and history informs us that Eochaid, the king, married the princess, with the consent of the prophet, providing he would renounce his false religion and worship the God of the Hebrews.

We follow the long line of Irish kings and queens down through the centuries, until the kingdom is overthrown to Scotland, and from Scotland down through the ages, until we see its final overthrow to England, which fulfills the prophecy of Ezekiel, viz.: "I will overturn, overturn, overturn it, and it shall be no more until he comes whose right it is, and I will give it to him," and in fulfillment of this very prophecy, we find the kingdom overturned from Jerusalem to Ireland, once; from Ireland to Scotland, twice; and from Scotland to England, three times, whose right it is.

Thus we trace the genealogy of Queen Victoria back to Zedekiah, the king of Jerusalem, "for know ye not that God made a covenant with David, by a pinch of salt, that the seed of Judah should reign over the house of Israel forever."

Oliver Cromwell was called to the throne by England, and never knew till the day of his death why he
refused the sceptre. The reason was, he belonged to
the tribe of Manasseh. The coronation stone is one of
the curiosities of Westminster Abbey. It is underneath
the coronation chair, and all of the kings and queens
of England, Scotland, and Ireland have been crowned
upon it, from Tea Tephi to Victoria. This is Bethel,
or Jacob's Pillar, and was carried from Jerusalem to
Ireland by Jeremiah and Baruch at the time they
planted the second empire. The ark of the covenant
they hid until Judah shall go before Israel into Jerusalem and acknowledge Christ as king.

If we examine some of the prophecies concerning
Manasseh we shall find them truly wonderful. God
had said to this thirteenth tribe of the children of
Israel that He would guard them as the eagle guardeth
her young, and so when they settled down to independ-
ence they placed the eagle upon their banner with
thirteen stars. They filled it up with the stripes, for it
is written, "by His stripes are we healed."

The great seal of the United States is still more curious. This was suggested by Sir John Bart, an Englishman, to John Adams, American Minister to the Court
of St. James, and adopted by Congress in 1782. On
the obverse side we have an eagle, and in his beak a
scroll, with the motto, "E. Pluribus Unum," one out of
many, as Manasseh was taken. Over the head of the

eagle is a bank of clouds, and we have the prophecy, " I will be a cloud round about you, in camp and out." There is a parting in the cloud, and we see thirteen stars, or the number of the tribe. In his right talon is an olive branch, a symbol of peace, and in his left talon a bundle of thirteen arrows. If we turn the seal over and look at the reverse side, we find it still more wonderful, for here we have the Egyptian pyramid. Over the top of the pyramid is an all-seeing eye, with the motto, " He prospers our beginning." Under the pyramid is the motto, " A new era in the ages." Now, when we come to think that Manasseh, the thirteenth tribe, which is represented on our flag and on our great seal, was born in Memphis, at the foot of the pyramids, we cannot fail to see how wonderfully prophecy and providence agree.

The prophecies concerning Israel were that they should possess the gates of their enemies; they should reign over many nations, but no nation should reign over them; they should have the heathen for an inheritance; they should be a Sabbath-keeping people; they should take their national oath in the name of the Lord; they should preach the gospel to every nation, kindred, tongue, and people, and that they should finally join hands with Judah to possess Palestine. There are but two nations on earth to-day that meet all of these requirements, viz., England and the United States. England has never been conquered by a Gentile power. They hold the gates of their enemies from Gibraltar to the China Sea.

Lord Wellington, with a small army, withstood nearly the entire forces of the Continent. They prevailed against Russia in the Crimean war; they opened the ports of China, with her 450,000,000; while heathen India, with her 250,000,000, comes under the British flag; and with her fifty-six colonies, the Dominion of Canada, the Feejee Islands, and her own islands, she owns nearly one-quarter of the entire earth and controls one-sixth of all the inhabitants. And yet, mighty as England was and is, she found her armies too weak to conquer the half-clothed, half-fed Pilgrims and Puritans that had entered the promised land, and had raised their banner in the name of the Lord.

Again, England's coat of arms is nine lions and a unicorn. The unicorn was added when the Norman conquerors invaded England, which are supposed to be the tribe of Benjamin. "For then will I turn the people to a pure language, that they may worship God with one consent." There are six languages in the Christian world to-day that are powerful, viz., English, Russian, German, French, Spanish, and Italian; but transplant any of them, except the English language, and they will die. Look at the vast sea of cosmopolitan languages that have been transplanted to the United States, and where are they now? They sleep the sleep that knows no resurrection, for the children cannot speak the mother tongue. In the English language we have about one thousand Hebrew roots, and hence it is written, "With stammering lips, and in another tongue, will He speak to His people."

Sharon Turner, in his "History of the Anglo-Saxons," says: "The Anglo-Saxons made their appearance in Media seven centuries before Christ; but that, according to Herodotus, Media was not their cradle, but Palestine." And he adds: "My sole object is to give a true solution to the difficult question, Who were the ancestors of the Anglo-Saxons?" This is an important point, from the fact that in tracing the Saxons back to Media, we find it to be the exact place and time that the house of Israel went into the Assyrian captivity, and if we call to our aid some of the ancient writers, we can prove that the Saxons came from that part of the country where Israel was lost, and that our forefathers occupied the northwestern part of Asia in the days of Christ, and that He sent His disciples into these very places to declare unto them freedom from the Mosaic law.

After the Israelites were carried into the Assyrian captivity, they remained in Media until Christ came, for you remember He said to His disciples, "Go not into the ways of the Gentiles, nor into any of the cities of the Samaritans enter ye not, but go rather to the lost sheep of the house of Israel," which fulfills the prophecy, "Yet doth He devise means that His banished be not

expelled from Him." From Media they went into
Pamphylia, Galatia, Cappadocia, Lydia, and Bithyania,
for we have the testimony of Josephus in the year 70
A.D., that the two tribes, viz., Judah and Levi, were
captured by Titus, but the ten tribes were beyond the
river Euphrates, an immense number of people. Here
they waited redemption from the Mosaic law. Christ's
mission on earth was to redeem Israel, for He says, " I
am not sent, but unto the lost sheep of the house of
Israel."

Under the Mosaic law Paul finds them, and tells
them of a crucified and risen Redeemer, and frees
them from the law. This is why we are keeping the
first day instead of the seventh. Again Paul tells them
to avoid foolish questions and genealogies, and endless
fables, and from that point of time they lose all trace
of their genealogy and become a distinct people. Thus
we see prophecy fulfilled to the letter of the law, viz.:
Unknown in name, speaking another tongue; in fact,
the little stone, cut out of the mountain without hands,
which became a great mountain, and filled the whole
earth.   THE AUTHOR.

The works examined, to which I am deeply in-
debted, are Herodotus, Josephus, Rollins, Chambers,
Hine and the voluminous parts of the " Heir of the
World," from which the pages of this Preface were
compiled.

AUTHOR'S PREFACE.

A LARGE majority of church members to-day were accepted by those bodies on a profession of faith while in their youth, and hence it arises that the Bible has become a neglected book, simply because the people have accepted the teachings of their pastors and Sabbath-school teachers, without a thorough examination into all of the laws and the prophets concerning Judah and Israel. These have been spiritualized by them until they have to a large extent lost their true meaning; while the commentaries, by their inaccuracies, have become, like old medical works, worse than useless.

Instead then of accepting any author as a guide, go directly to the Scriptures, and, like an astronomer, carefully weigh in the balance every thought put forth by the prophets, and thereby become a commentary unto yourselves (1) 1 Thes: v. 20. I have examined the Scriptures carefully, and append the following preface, giving the distinctions which exist between the house of Judah and the house of Israel. Israel was to be "unknown in name" (2) Is. lxv. 15. "A multitudinous people" (3) Hos. i. 10. "Strong in power" (4) Is. xli. 12. "An island nation having large colonies" (5) Is. xli. 1–8, and "A Christian people" (6) Rom. ix. 4. Judah

was to be "without a government" (7) Jer. xvii. 4.
"Strangers tolerated in all foreign countries" (8) Jer.
xv. 4. "Under the Mosaic law" (9) Rom. ii. 17, and
"should always be known as a curse," while Israel, "his
servant, should be called by another name" (10) Is.
lxv. 15.

It will be noticed, secondly, that the Commandments
were given to Israel, and that wherever she is found she
must be found with not only her church but also her
government founded upon them. St. Paul says, "When
the Gentiles who have not the law" (11) Rom. ii. 14,
proving conclusively that we are not Gentiles, because
we have the law, and not only that, but our government is based on all of the laws embodied in the Ten
Commandments.

In giving testimony in a court, we take our oath in
the name of the Lord (12) Ex. xxii. 11, and again we
were charged not to give false evidence (13) Ex. xxiii. 1.
So England and the United States swear in court to
give the truth, the whole truth, and nothing but the
truth, so help them God, and also make perjury a state
prison offense. Israel went into the Assyrian captivity, from which they have never returned (14) 2 Kings
xvii. 23. Judah did return as seen by (15) Neh. vii. 6.
Israel lost her genealogy (16) Titus iii. 9, and remained
under the law until John (17) Luke xvi. 16, and then
went away to an island home to establish a kingdom (18)
Is. xlii. 10–12, (19) Jer. xxxi. 10.

The islands would become too small, and they would
lose Manasseh (20) Is. xlix. 20. They should push the
people to the ends of the earth, as in the case of the
American Indians (21) Deut. xxxiii. 17, and should be
saved through Christ (22) Rom. xi. 26. Again, Judah
should always reign over Israel (23) Ps. cxxxii. 11, (24)
2 Chron. xiii. 5, xxi. 7. Ephraim must be a multitude
of nations, while Manasseh would become a great people
(25) Gen. xlviii. 19, they should possess the gates of
their enemies (26) Gen. xxiv. 60. They should never
be conquered (27) Is. xli. 8–12. They should have the
heathen for an inheritance (28) Ps. cv. 44. Christ was
not sent, but unto the lost sheep of the house of Israel
(29) Matt. xv. 24, while all of her children must be
taught of the Lord (30) Is. liv. 13. Wherefore the children of Israel shall keep the Sabbath for a sign between
me and them (31) Ex. xxxi. 17.

Again, wherever we find the quail and honey-bee,
there we find Israel, as they are as distinctly marked
out for Israel as the frog and locust were for Egypt.
God brought the quail to Israel while they wandered
in the wilderness, and the whole country was filled with
wild honey. So in like manner the quail and honey-bee
follow the Anglo-Saxon, and will go no farther than he
goes. Not until the first white man crossed the Mis-
souri river would the first swarm of bees cross. " Thus
it came to pass, that when the Indians saw a bee, they
went home to their wigwams to sound the alarm. The

white man is among us, and we must leave the graves of our fathers and depart." These are God's witnesses for signs and for wonders, and belong to Israel only. Books might be written upon the identification of the lost sheep of the house of Israel and the Anglo-Saxons, but I leave the reader to examine the Scriptures carefully, after which "let every one be fully persuaded in his own mind."

SCRIPTURAL REFERENCES.

(1) Thess. v. 20—"Despise not prophesyings."

(2) Is. lxv. 15—"And ye shall leave your name for a curse unto my chosen; for the Lord God shall slay thee, and call His servants by another name."

(3) Hos. i. 10.—"Yet the number of the children of Israel shall be as the sands of the sea, which cannot be measured nor numbered; and it shall come to pass, that in the place where it was said unto them, 'Ye are not my people,' there it shall be said unto them, 'Ye are the sons of the living God.'"

(4) Is. xli. 12—"They that war against thee, shall be as nothing, and as a thing of naught."

(5) Is. xli. 1–8—"Keep silence before me, O islands, and let the people renew their strength." "But thou, Israel, art my servant, Jacob whom I have chosen, the seed of Abraham, my friend."

(6) Rom. ix. 4—"Who are Israelites, to whom pertaineth the adoption, and the glory, and the covenants,

and the giving of the law, and the service of God, and
the promises."

(7) Jer. xvii. 4—" And thou, even thyself, shalt discon-
tinue from thine heritage, that I gave thee; and I will
cause thee to serve thine enemies, in the land which
thou knowest not; for ye have kindled a fire in mine
anger which shall burn forever."

(8) Jer. xv. 4—"And I will cause them to be removed into all kingdoms of the earth."

(9) Rom. ii. 17—"Behold, thou art called a Jew, and
restest in the law."

(10) Is. lxv. 15—"And ye shall leave your name for
a curse unto my chosen; for the Lord God shall slay
thee, and call His servants by another name."

(11) Rom. ii. 14—"For when the Gentiles which
have not the law."

(12) Ex. xxii. 11—"Then shall an oath of the Lord
be between them both."

(13) Ex. xxiii. 1—"Thou shalt not raise a false
report; put not thine hand with the wicked to be an
unrighteous witness."

(14) 2 Kings xvii. 23—"So was Israel carried away
out of their own land to Assyria unto this day."

(15) Neh. vii. 6—"These are the children of the
province that went up out of the captivity of those that
had been carried away; whom Nebuchadnezzar, the
King of Babylon, had carried away, and to Judah, every
one unto his own city."

(16) Titus iii. 9—"But avoid foolish questions and genealogies, and contentions, and striving about the law."

(17) Luke xvi. 16—"The law and the prophets were until John."

(18) Is. xlii. 12—"Let them give glory unto the Lord and declare His praise in the islands."

(19) Jer. xxxi. 10—"Hear the word of the Lord, O ye nations, and declare it in the isles afar off, and say, 'He that scattered Israel will gather him, and keep him as a shepherd doth his flock.'"

(20) Is. xlix. 20—"The children which thou shalt have after thou hast lost the other, shall say again in thine ears, 'The place is too strait for me; give place to me that I may dwell.'"

(21) Deu. xxxiii. 17—"His glory is like the firstling of his bullock, and his horns are like the horns of unicorns, with them he shall push the people together to the ends of the earth, and they are the ten thousands of Ephraim, and they are the thousands of Manasseh."

(22) Rom. xi. 26—"And so all Israel shall be saved."

(23) Ps. cxxxii. 11—"The Lord hath sworn in truth unto David He will not turn from it; of the fruit of thy body will I set upon thy throne."

(24) 2 Chron. xiii. 5; xxi. 7—"Ought ye not to know that the Lord God of Israel gave the kingdom over Israel to David forever, even to him and to his sons by a covenant of salt." "Howbeit the Lord

would not destroy the house of David, because of the covenant that He had made with David, and as He promised to give a light to him and to his sons forever."

(25) Gen. xlviii. 19—"And his father refused, and said, 'I know it, my son, I know it; he also shall become a people, and he also shall be great; but truly his younger brother shall be greater than he, and his seed shall become a multitude of nations."

(26) Gen. xxiv. 60—"And let thy seed possess the gate of those which hate them."

(27) Is. xli. 8–12—"But thou, Israel, are my servant." "Fear thou not, for I am with thee." "They that strive with thee shall perish." "They that war with thee shall be as nothing and as a thing of naught."

(28) Ps. cv. 44—"And gave them the lands of the heathen, and they inherited the labor of the people."

(29) Matt. xv. 24—"But He answered and said, 'I am not sent but unto the lost sheep of the house of Israel.'"

(30) Is. liv. 13—"And all thy children shall be taught of the Lord; and great shall be the peace of thy children."

(31) Ex. xxxi. 17—"It is a sign between me, and the children of Israel forever; for in six days the Lord made heaven and earth, and on the seventh He rested, and was refreshed."

———

In Matthew's Bible, published at Antwerp in 1740,

we find in the second chapter of the second book of Chronicles the following verse:

"And now I have sent a wyse man, and a man of understandynge, called Hiram Abi, and is the sonne of a woman of the daughters of Dan, whobeit, hys father was a Tirian."

Coverdale's Bible, of 1535, speaks of him as Abif, hence we can see at a glance that the craft has retained the correct name.

MORTAL—IMMORTAL.

Herodotus tells us that prior to Menes, King of Egypt, the world was governed by immortals. This statement is borne out by the Genesis history of creation, as the sixth chapter of Genesis proves conclusively that the flood (which was universal) came to pass through the intermarriage of mortal with immortal. These are distinguished as the Sons of God and the daughters of men. The Sons of God are known in the Scriptures as children born to Adam after the so-called fall of man, for upon the birth of Cain (the first child born unto her after the transgression), Eve exclaimed, "I have gotten a man from the Lord"; and again at the birth of Seth she said, "God hath appointed me another seed instead of Abel, whom Cain slew." This fact is again borne out by the language of the Almighty, who exclaims, "Behold, the man is become as one of us, to know good and evil." Man has

now passed from immortal to mortal, and immediately
a Saviour is promised, which elevates them to the sublime position of being designated as the Sons of God.
Prior to that time the earth was densely inhabited
by the posterity of Adam and Eve, and were immortal,
in the fact that they were void of knowledge, and of a
sense of right or wrong, and death had not been pronounced upon them, in that man had not sinned.

This is proven by the fact that Adam called his
wife's name Eve, because she was the mother of all the
living; and again Cain says, "It shall come to pass
that every one that findeth me shall slay me." From
this race Cain took his wife; consequently, we came
through the loins of Seth. From the day of Adam's
transgression to the day of his death was 930 years.
Prior to that time he may have lived for thousands of
years, as no age can be assigned to immortality. We
have now two distinct races: mortal and immortal,
and hence it follows that the intermarriage produced
a race, with death and without death; with the law
and without the law; with a Redeemer and without a
Redeemer, and this state of affairs brought forth from
Job the exclamation, "Now, what can the Almighty
do for them?"

Again they became a race of serpent worshipers,
as can be proven by the construction of their mounds
throughout the earth; and again Job says, "Hast
thou marked the old way which wicked men have

trodden, whose foundations were overthrown with a
flood?" David says, "I have said ye were gods, but
ye shall die like men." Hence, the first command-
ment, "Thou shalt have no other gods before Me,"
was *apropos* to that period. After the crucifixion of
Christ they ceased to become the torments of men.
In 1st Peter iii. 19, 20, we find the proof of this.
"By which, also, He went and preached unto the
spirits in prison, which sometime were disobedient,
when once the long-suffering of God waited in the days
of Noah, while the ark was preparing, wherein few, that
is eight souls, were saved by water." Hence, being
baptized by water, means obedience to Christ.

(*Thau.*)   MASONRY.   (*Triad.*)

Masonry was founded upon the great fiat of the
Almighty, "Let there be light, and there was light."
It was founded upon the sacred number three, which
extends back into eternity, and carries us on the waves
of time forward toward eternal progression. When God
the Father, Son, and Spirit called into existence the
great solar and stellar system, He divided the hundreds
of millions of stars that He had created into triangles,
each three being a trinity in themselves. When He
created the earth, He also created two great lights, the
greater light to rule the day and the lesser light to rule
the night. He divided the world into three distinct
elements, viz., earth, air, and water. He called into existence three states of matter, viz., animal, vegetable,

and mineral. He created man, and endowed him with soul, body, and spirit.

Masonry is represented by the Holy Bible, square, and compasses. The oracles were transmitted to Shem, Ham, and Japhet; thence to Abraham, Isaac, and Jacob; thence to King Solomon, Hiram king of Tyre, and Hiram Abif; still onward to the final secretion of the ark of the covenant by Jeremiah the prophet, Baruch the blessed, and Eochaid the prince.

Again, masonry is divided into three grand divisions, viz., Lodge, Chapter, and Commandery. These are divided into three degrees each.

We begin, first, by bearing an uncut piece of granite from the quarry; second, by bearing the ark of the covenant; and, third, by bearing the cross. We look on Calvary, and we behold Christ dying between two thieves; again we look, and we see Him traveling toward Emmaus between two disciples; but in the third and most sublime degree, we see three men, Peter and John and James, behold the glory of Our Lord, for now He is standing on the Mount of Transfiguration between two saints—Moses, to represent the law, and Elias, the prophets. Hence the parable, " If they hear not Moses and the prophets, neither will they be persuaded, though one rose from the dead." "Sun, moon, and stars, pyramid, tabernacle, temple; Shem, Job, Melchizedek, man, angel, Christ, Father, Son, and Spirit." "So mote it be."

THE IRISH PRINCE AND HEBREW PROPHET.

CHAPTER I.

JEREMIAH.

The Pit.

IN a dark, narrow dungeon, underneath the king's palace in Jerusalem, two men had been confined for treason against the Jewish kingdom. These men had been especially ordained by God to tear down, through a long and eventful career, and at its close to build again, the kingdom of a lost and nameless race. Prior to this time there had been two others who had in their youth cried out against the Jews, and they also had been carried into captivity; hence, it came to pass that, at the opening of this story, the four men were all confined within the walls of their captors. The two who were confined in the prison at Jerusalem were Jeremiah the prophet and Baruch the blessed. The two who were in captivity under Nebuchadnezzar were Daniel, who was in Babylon, and Ezekiel, who was in Mesopotamia.

For years prior to this time Jeremiah had been persecuted by the kings of Jerusalem, because he had urged them to deal honorably with Nebuchadnezzar,

the king of Babylon, and thus save the city and temple
from destruction.   But they had not only beaten him,
but cast him into prison; and from his confinement the
word of the Lord came unto him, which was recorded
by his faithful scribe, and immediately transmitted to
the king.   "Now when Jehudi had read three or four
leaves, he cut it with his penknife, and cast it into the
fire."   Again the word of the Lord came to the Seer,
and again he commanded Baruch to write, saying, "The
king of Babylon shall certainly come, and destroy the
land, and shall cause to cease from thence man and
beast."

When Zedekiah became king, the word of the Lord
came again to Jeremiah, saying, "Thus saith the Lord,
He that remaineth in the city shall die by the sword,
by the famine, and by the pestilence; but he that
goeth forth to the Chaldeans shall live."   "Therefore
the princes (or king's sons) said unto the king, 'We beseech thee, let this man be put to death, for he weak-
eneth the hands of the men of war.'"   And hence there
arose a cry throughout all Jerusalem, "Death to the
traitor."   Baruch had finally been apprehended as an
accessory to the fact, and he too had been cast into the
dungeon with his Godly companion.

Within the city a strange and unusual commotion
agitated the people.   Zedekiah the king had formed
an unholy alliance with the king of Egypt; he had
broken faith with Nebuchadnezzar, insomuch that

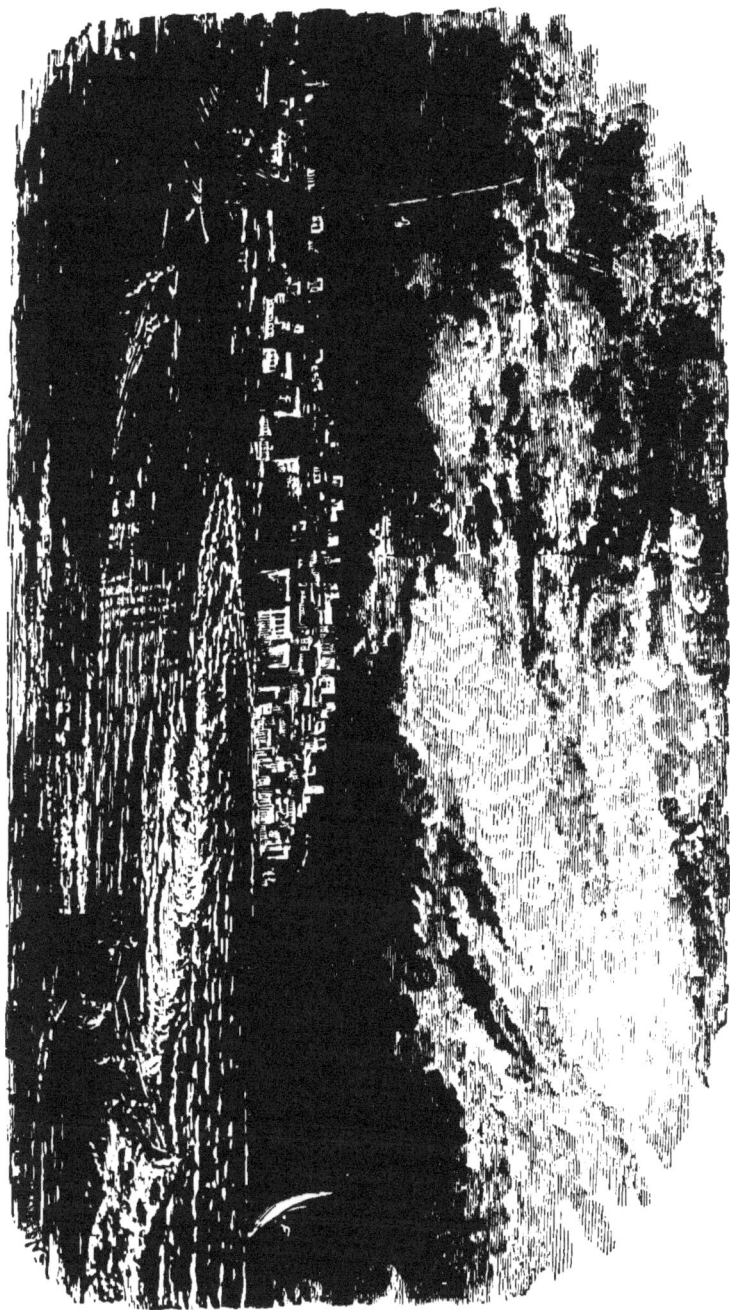

JOPPA.

Jerusalem was encompassed by the Chaldean hosts, and had been in a state of siege for eighteen months. To add to the horror of the situation, famine and pestilence were rampant throughout the city, destroying the Jews by the thousands; and to make the situation still more deplorable, the bodies of the victims all had to be entombed within the walls of the city.

"This is the last day of the eighteenth month since our city has been encompassed by the Chaldeans," said Baruch, after the door of the dungeon had closed upon them.

"'Tis well," said Jeremiah. "The end is at hand. Had our king obeyed the voice of the prophets, Jerusalem might have been saved, but now, alas, it is too late; the city will be destroyed, the temple burned, and the holy vessels carried away to Babylon."

"Good faith," said Baruch, "our king little dreams of the power of the monarch of Babylon, else he would not urge the people on to combat. God hath revealed to me these three years past that Judah is on the borders of its death-struggle, and that Zedekiah is its last king."

"But," said Jeremiah, "know ye not that God made a covenant with David, by a pinch of salt, that the seed of Judah should reign over the house of Israel forever?"

"I know," said Baruch, "that we read it in the Holy Parchment; but where are they now? Since the day they went into the Assyrian captivity, they have been as completly lost as though they had never existed."

"That is true, and will remain true, till all things are fulfilled, for they were to lose their name and identity, speak another tongue, and evangelize the world; and Ezekiel, who is crying aloud in his captivity in Mesopotamia, says that this can be accomplished only after they have been overthrown three distinct times.

"'But the day cometh, saith the Lord, that I will bring again the captivity of my people Israel and Judah, saith the Lord, and I will cause them to return to the land that I gave to their fathers, and they shall possess it.' Isaiah prophesied more than one hundred years ago that they would have an island home, establish again a kingdom, and be as in the days of our fathers Abraham, Isaac, and Jacob, a God-fearing people. He also prophesied that a man called Cyrus would rise up and liberate the Jews."

"Ah, Isaiah was grand even in death. My grandfather stood by his side on the morning of his execution. On that morning he was one hundred years old, and he exclaimed, 'Trust ye in the Lord forever, for in the Lord Jehovah is everlasting strength.' This was reported to Manasseh as high treason. The king abhorred his oracle, and ordered him sawn asunder. In that same hour the Assyrian hosts swooped down upon the city, and Manasseh was taken prisoner, bound in fetters, and carried captive into Babylon."

I have often thought it would have been a grand sight to have seen Isaiah, Amos, and Hosea, in King Hezekiah's palace on the morning that he brought them together, to sanctify the house of the Lord. The Lord brought Judah low because of Ahaz, the king. He persecuted the prophets, cut in pieces the holy vessels of the temple, and shut the doors of the house of our God.

"And what think you," said Baruch, "will become of our temple, and the holy vessels, if the Czar forces the walls?"

"The temple will be burned, and the vessels carried to Babylon. A curse will follow the Jews forever. They will always be known as Jews, never losing their name nor identity. They will remain under the Mosaic law, be without a government, and strangers tolerated in all foreign countries, while Israel will be unknown in name, speaking another tongue, many mighty nations, and a religious people, with the Lion of the tribe of Judah as their leader, for the Israelite Hosea has already prophesied 'That it shall come to pass, that in the place where it was said "ye are not my people," there it shall be said, "ye are the sons of the living God."

"Good faith," said Baruch. "I believe that if the Lion of the tribe of Judah came to-day, he would be cast into prison, and condemned to death without a trial."

"When Shiloh comes," said Jeremiah, "he must come through the seed of David. He will come to his own, but they will not receive him. He will then go to the lost sheep of the house of Israel. While they are lost to us through the Assyrian captivity, they will be found by him, and freed from the Mosaic law. But hark! hear ye not the tramp of soldiers coming down the passage?"

At this moment the door of the dungeon was thrown open and four men entered the cell. The foremost one amongst them carried a taper in one hand and a strong cord in the other. In the southeast corner of the prison was a deep pit, wherein was mire and dirt. Seizing the prophet, they drew him to the edge of the pit, then fastening the cord under his arms they lowered him down, down. O God! Will the bottom never be reached? Yes, at last, for they feel the cord yield, until they are sure that Jeremiah has sunk to rise no more. Then they throw the cord in after him and depart, leaving Baruch alone.

As soon as the echo of the footsteps of this band of murderers had died away, Baruch arose and felt his way cautiously towards the mouth of the pit. The light the soldiers had carried blinded his eyes, and now the darkness was so great it could almost be felt. Carefully he crept along on his hands and knees, until he could feel the side of the chasm; then, leaning over as far as he dared, he called out, "Jeremiah." There was no answer. Silence, like that of the tomb, had now taken possession of the dungeon, that only a few moments ago was a house of prayer. Thinking his companion was dead, he broke forth into loud lamentations. Again he listened, and soon he heard, coming up from the bowels of the earth, his own name:

" Baruch."

Again he strains every nerve to catch the faintest sound that might come to him, as an oracle from Jehovah.

" Baruch!"

" Here am I."

" I am in a horrible pit of miry clay. I am sunk up to my arm-pits, and if I move to free myself I sink deeper. My hands are spread out to increase the surface, as I have somewhat to say. Are you alone?"

" Yes."

" You are sure no one can hear me but yourself?"

" Yes."

" Then I charge you to look well to the Princess Tea Tephi, the youngest daughter of Zedekiah. Her mother was the daughter of Zephaniah, the prophet, and through her the true line of the house of Judah will be saved. God hath revealed to me that the princess will be saved alive—and, Baruch. The ark of the covenant—"

" Hist! Some one approaches."

The door of the cell was unlocked and pushed open, and the woolly head of a stalwart Ethiopian peered into the gloom. Behind him marched thirty men, who had been commanded by the king to rescue the prophet from the pit. Holding his taper over the chasm, and drawing a strong cord whereon was a noose from underneath his tunic, he stooped down and bade Jeremiah adjust it under his arms. In this manner he was taken up from the horrible pit, and miry clay, and his feet placed upon a rock. The Ethiopian then bade the prophet follow him, and he was led down through the corridor to a court in the prison, wherein was a bath and a change of raiment. The key turned in the lock, and he was alone.

The morning after his escape from the pit, while he was in prayer, his door was opened by the Ethiopian, who summoned him before the king. Jeremiah knew that Zedekiah feared the Jews, and he was at a loss to understand by what means, or to whose authority, he owed his wonderful escape. He had heard the Jews cry out, "Death to the traitor!" when he was urging them to surrender to the Chaldean monarch and save their families alive.

Zedekiah stood in fear of the prophet, as well as the people, for well he knew that he was inspired, and that he had trampled his inspirations under foot. But now the time had come when he must inquire of God, through one of the prophets.

As the Seer was led by the Ethiopian into the third
entry of the temple, fear came upon the face of the
king. Before him stood God's anointed. Would he
condemn him and his family to death?

"Jeremiah," said the king, "our city has been encompassed and in a state of siege for eighteen months.
We are groveling in the dust before two other mon-
archs. They are pestilence and famine. What shall I
do to appease the anger of the Lord?"

"Have you humbled yourself in the dust before
God?" asked the prophet.

The king trembled, but answered him nothing.

"Then," said Jeremiah after a moment's pause, "deliver up the city into the hands of Nebuchadnezzar, and
your lives will be spared and the city saved. Disobey,
and the city will be thrown down from the foundation
stones, the temple will be burned, your sons will be
killed, and you will be bound, hand and foot, in fetters
of brass, with sightless orbs carried away captive into
Babylon. Escape now, ere it be everlastingly too
late."

The king stood with bowed head during this recital.
He would gladly follow the advice of the Seer, but alas!
he feared the Jews. What would his sons say if he
ordered the gates to be thrown open? They would
curse him to his face. It must not be. The siege must
be endured to the end, for God was a God of the Jews
and not of the Gentiles. No, rather a thousand deaths

than the betrayal of his countrymen. Raising his eyes, he commanded that the prophet be conducted back to the court.

As the Seer stood alone once more, his thoughts went back over the past twenty-four hours. God had indeed mercifully preserved him, and he knew it was for some wise purpose. Was he ordained by God to be the instrument in His hands of setting up the second empire? He knew, as Grand Chaplain of the Mystic Brotherhood, that should the Czar force the walls the ark would be immediately hid. No nation should ever possess it, should ever handle it, should ever see it, save that kingdom that was governed by the true seed of the house of David. It must be secreted on Israel-itish soil.

But where are they? Oh, that we might find them and bury these precious mementos of the loving kind-ness of our God beneath their treasure-house, to be kept in remembrance by our brotherhood to the final hour, when Judah should go before Israel into Jerusa-lem. " Hark! Was that the thundering of the tem-pest or the roar of the chariot wheels? Great God! the hour has come, the walls of Jerusalem have fallen."

CHAPTER II.

THE city of Jerusalem at this time had three walls wherever it was not impassable by valley, but wherever these gorges occurred it had but one. It was built upon four hills, which were called Mount Zion, Moriah, Acra and BEZETHA. The temple stood upon Moriah, while the palace occupied Mount Zion. The principal valley was called Siloam, which by interpretation means "Sweet Water." The outsides of the four hills were surrounded by deep valleys, and by means of these precipices were everywhere impassable; consequently, there was but one wall, which was built by David and Solomon, who were exceedingly particular about the strength of this fortification.

The second wall began at the gate Gennath and encompassed the whole northern part of the city. The third wall began at the tower Hippicus, passing on beyond the sepulchres of the kings to the monument of the Fuller and joined the old wall in the valley of Cedron.

The old wall, with its battlements and turrets, was 37 feet high and 30 feet broad, built of square stone, as

(43)

solid as the wall itself. In these towers were chambers of great magnificence. On the third wall were ninety of these towers, on the middle wall forty, and on the old one sixty. The third wall was the strongest and most magnificent, being 105 feet high, and from the summit Arabia was plainly to be seen as well as the whole possessions of the Hebrews from the Mediterranean Sea westward. The whole compass of the city was 33 furlongs, and it was considered impregnable against all of the hosts of the Eastern empires.

The temple was the grandest house ever erected on earth, and hence the pride of the Jews. On three sides, beginning in the valley, the walls were four hundred and fifty.feet high, built of the purest marble, cut in blocks from thirty to sixty feet long, and from fifteen to twenty feet broad. There were engaged in building this magnificent temple to our God "thirty thousand men, who worked by courses of ten thousand per month. Among the cedars of Lebanon there were seventy thousand who bore burdens, and there were eighty thousand stone cutters in the quarries. Over these were three thousand three hundred officers."

This building was fashioned so nicely in the quarries, and among the cedars, "that there was neither hammer nor axe, nor any other tool of iron heard in the house while it was building." It covered twelve acres of ground, which represented the twelve tribes of the children of Israel. The oracle for the reception of the ark of the covenant was thirty feet long, thirty feet broad, and thirty feet high, overlaid with pure gold. The floor was laid with plates of gold; in fact, the whole house, both within and without, was overlaid with gold. In the oracle were two cherubims, each fifteen feet high, with wings seven and a half feet outstretched, so that each wing touched the other at the centre and the wall on either side. These were overlaid with pure gold, as was also the whole room, both floor and ceiling, together with the walls, the whole being carved with palm trees, pomegranates, flowers, and lilies. "Moreover, he made a great throne of ivory, and overlaid it with pure gold, while twelve lions in pure gold, of life size, stood upon the six steps and round about the throne."

This cunning craftsmanship was from the subtle hands of our Grand Master, Hiram king of Tyre, whose father was a Tyrian, and whose widowed mother was an Israelite of the house of Naphtali, and Hiram Abif, whose father was a Tyrian, and whose widowed mother was an Israelite of the house of Dan.

"These were all made according to the will of Solomon."

There were two pillars of brass, more beautiful and more valuable than any of the golden ornaments. The height was twenty-seven feet, and the circumference eighteen feet. There were small palms made of brass, covered with lily work, to which were hung two hun-

dred pomegranates in two rows, hanging from the top
to the bottom of each pillar. These were placed at the
entrance of the porch, the one on the right and the
other on the left. They were named Jachin and Boaz,
which denoted strength and beauty. The network of
lilies and pomegranates denoted unity, peace and plenty.
There were seven golden steps leading up between
these two pillars and the outer court, which had written
in letters of brass seven distinct interpretations, viz.,
the seven Sabbatical years; the seven wonders of the
world; the seven years of famine; the seven years of
plenty; the seven planets; the seven sciences, viz.,
grammar, rhetoric, logic, arithmetic, geometry, music,
and astronomy; and, lastly, the seven years occupied
in building the temple.

The ark of the covenant was placed on the ivory
throne in the oracle. This was made by Bezaleel,
under the supervision of Moses and Aaron. It was
three feet nine inches long, two feet three inches broad,
and two feet three inches high. It was overlaid within
and without with pure gold, with a crown of gold round
about it. There were also four golden rings in each
corner. Within the ark were the two stone tablets,
whereon was written, by the hand of Moses, the Ten
Commandments. Standing in front of the throne was
the grand golden table whereon were the loaves of God.

"There were also ten thousand golden candlesticks,
with candles that burned day and night, round about

the throne, while twenty thousand golden censers carried incense to the throne, and fifty thousand carried
fire.

"There were ten thousand priests, two hundred thousand trumpeters, and two hundred thousand singers.

"Attached to the temple was the equery, which contained one thousand four hundred golden chariots.
twelve thousand horsemen, and forty and four thousand
stalls."

The immensity of the temple can only be conceived
by considering the tremendous height of the walls, the
number of its stories, and a twelve-acre surface to each
story.

"On that day when the temple was burned there
had been twenty-one kings over Israel, for a period of
five hundred and fourteen years, six months, and ten
days.

"It was burned four hundred and seventy years, six
months, and ten days after being dedicated; one thousand and sixty-two years, six months, and ten days from
the exodus of the children of Israel out of Egypt; one
thousand nine hundred and fifty-seven years, six months,
and ten days from the deluge; and three thousand five
hundred and thirteen years, six months, and ten days
from Adam."

Zedekiah sat on the throne on that, the tenth and
last day, the last king that should rule over Judah until
all things should be fulfilled.

When Jeremiah heard the walls of Jerusalem fall, he sprang up to the grated window of the new cell, where he had been taken after being rescued from the pit, and, taking a silver trumpet from beneath his robe, gave seven distinct blasts. This was answered back by three times three. To this the Seer answered by three.

Nearly an hour passed away, while the prophet stood clinging to the bars of the cell, straining every nerve to catch the welcome sound of the silver trumpet he knew so well. It must be hid; God would not allow it to fall into the hands of the Babylonian monarch. At last he hears the trumpeter give seven blasts. He immediately answers back with three times three, and receives the welcome three. Then he knows that the ark is hid by the mystic seven, who will keep it in remembrance for all time ; and from that hour the Jews will say, " No more the ark of the covenant of the Lord, neither shall it come to mind, neither shall they remember it, neither shall they visit it, neither shall that be done any more."

" Oh, ye Jews, your ark has passed from your keeping, till the blast of the silver trumpet shall call your scattered remnant back to Jerusalem, to witness the fulfillment of all the laws and prophets concerning Israel." " Then shall ye look on Calvary." " Then shall the trumpet sound." "May the God of our fathers, Abraham, Isaac, and Jacob, sustain you until that hour."

Thus spake the prophet, while to his ears came the roar of the chariot wheels, the thundering of the tempest, the blast of the trumpets, the shrill commands of the victors, the shrieks and groans of the dying as they were trampled under foot by the horsemen or cut down by the swordsmen.

"O Jerusalem, Jerusalem, thou that killest the prophets and stonest them which are sent unto thee, how often would I have gathered thy children together, even as a hen gathereth her chickens under her wings, but ye would not. Behold your house is left unto you desolate."

Within the royal palace all was confusion. The prophecies of Jeremiah were like thorns piercing the brain and heart of the king. The royal family had been gathered together preparatory to a hasty departure, but where, oh where, was Myra and the beautiful princess Tea Tephi, the pet and the pride of the king? Her mother was the daughter of Zephania, and through her all of the hopes of the king had been centered. She must be found at all hazards. "Away, and bring her before it is too late."

But hark! the enemy's troops have forced an entrance into the palace.

"Away, away!" Guided by the faithful Ethiopian, the family fled through the secret passages into the garden until they entered the ditches, and through them passed out of the city into the road leading to

Jericho.   The king looked back once only, to see the temple on fire, then he hastened on to meet his doom.

Within the city's walls a scene of desolation, carnage, ruin, and bloodshed, such as had never been witnessed before, was being enacted.   The Jews, already weakened by famine and pestilence, were in no condition to encounter the stalwart warriors of the Babylonish monarch.

Waving his sword on high, the captain of the host shouted the war cry, which was echoed back by his .victorious chieftains.

The Jews knew not where to fly for refuge.   The merchant prince and the beggar were now all at the mercy of the conqueror.   Resistance was useless against the fierce charge of the cavalry, who spared neither young nor old; all went down under the flashing swords and spears of the victorious hosts.   Every avenue of escape was now closed, while the streets were choked with the bodies of men, women, and children who had attempted to flee before the maddened throng.   The tempest which had come down upon the city when the walls fell was now sweeping the blood of the victims into the ditches, until there flowed out of Jerusalem rivers of blood.

The temple was pillaged, and now there went up a cloud of flame and smoke that carried consternation from the Sea of Galilee to the Dead Sea; yea, from the river Euphrates even unto the Mediterranean.

TOMB OF HIRAM ABIF.

At this moment a howl went up from the palace. "The king has escaped." "Pursue him," said the captain, and at the head of his cavalry they dashed out through the gates of the city toward Jericho. Onward they flew over the rocky and mountainous passes, while onward Zedekiah and his family were pressing. Could they reach Jericho?

"Too late!" They hear the shouts of the conquerors as they come thundering down the mountainous road, and then they hear the command, "Halt!"

"Alas, alas!" Why had he not heeded the words of Jeremiah? "Now it was too late." Swords flash on high, steel clashes steel, until they are all borne down and bound hand and foot, to be carried captive into Riblah.

And now the dethroned king is commanded to mount, and the whole body ride away, to enter into the presence of the Chaldean monarch, whom the fallen king had so ruthlessly betrayed. "Halt!" It was the voice of Nebuchadnezzar who thus commanded. "Die!" and at his command swords flash in the reddening glare of the western sunset, his wives, his sons, his daughters, all are swept out of time into the presence of Judah's God.

And now there comes the final scene that must be enacted to fulfill all the laws and the prophets, before Zedekiah is bound hand and foot, in fetters of brass, to be carried away into Babylon.

Look now, O ye king, for the last time over the land flowing with milk and with honey, that the Lord thy God gave to thy fathers for an inheritance. Look now, O king, towards Jerusalem, and behold the pyre of thy throne and the destruction of thy kingdom. Behold for the last time the glories of the universe and the wonderful works of the children of men. The sun sinks to rest, and as he looks his eyes are closed for ever.

CHAPTER III.

PALESTINE was bounded on the north by Syria, on the south by Edom, on the east by Bashan, and on the west by the Mediterranean Sea. Jerusalem was situated in Benjamin's territory, on the extreme west. It was bounded on the north by Ephraim, on the south by Judah, on the east by Benjamin, and on the west by Dan. Dan's territory ran west to the coast of the Mediterranean Sea, while Benjamin's extended east to the shores of the Dead Sea. The River Jordan connected the Sea of Galilee on the north with the Dead Sea on the south, being a straight line one from the other, about sixty miles, although the windings of the river made the distance very much farther. The distance from Jerusalem then to the Sea of Galilee was something over sixty miles. East of Jerusalem some twenty miles lay the Dead Sea, while directly south twenty miles lay Hebron, the home of Abraham.

Jericho lay in a northeasterly direction, being two hours' journey from Jordan and six hours' journey from Jerusalem. Southeast of the city lay Bethany, one-half hour's journey, while Bethlehem lay directly

(55)

south about five hours' journey. Northwest from Jerusalem lay Mizpah, a two hours' journey, on the road to
Lydda, and thence to Joppa, Lydda being situated
about half way between Joppa and Jerusalem. The
Mount of Olives was situated east-northeast from Jerusalem and commanded a magnificent view of the city
and surrounding country. Nazareth was situated in
Zebulon's territory, fifteen miles west of the Sea of
Galilee and sixty miles north of Jerusalem.

From the day that Israel went into the Assyrian
captivity up to the day that Jerusalem was taken by
Nebuchadnezzar was one hundred and thirty-seven
years, six months, and ten days!

When Jeremiah awoke the next morning after the
battle he experienced a sense of relief, in that Jerusalem had been taken by the Chaldean monarch. Already
Gedaliah had been appointed Governor over Jerusalem,
while thousands were being bound to be transported to
Babylon. The word of the Lord had come to Jeremiah during the night concerning Ebed Melech, the
Ethiopian, declaring him to be free, in that he had put
his trust in the Lord, and the Seer had determined in
his own mind that should he be liberated from prison
he would immediately take him under his care and
protection. He knew that he would prove faithful, even
unto death. He knew now that he owed his life to the
Ethiopian, for it had been revealed to him in a dream.
He saw him standing before Zedekiah, pleading for his

life and saying that the men had done evil who had cast him into the pit. He saw in his dream the countenance of the king change and he heard the command, " Take thirty men and rescue him."

Then the Lord revealed to him that He would not only spare the life of the Ethiopian, but He would make him an instrument of much good in the work of transplanting Judah over Israel. Then his thoughts went out after the princess. That she was in the city he had no doubt, but where was she lodging? Would she be treated as becomes the king's daughter, or would she be bound and cast into prison? He knew that Nebuchadnezzar would show no mercy towards any of the king's family, and if he heard that any of them were hid in Jerusalem he would set the hounds after them, and if necessary pursue them even unto the ends of the earth. But he would put his trust in the Lord. God would not forsake him nor bring his prophecies to naught. " Kings for time, but God for eternity." Nebuchadnezzar was God's servant, but he had yet to bow his neck to the yoke. The Son of God would appear to him in the fiery furnace and he would acknowledge that Jehovah ruled, but pride and vanity would send him forth for seven years to eat grass like the oxen before he would bow down before Israel's God.

Then bowing himself before his grated window he yielded himself up to prayer, and behold the flood-gates of the light of the New Jerusalem burst forth over the prison. The prophet was talking face to face with an angel of the Lord. There was a sound as of the rushing of mighty waters, the prison trembled from its foundation stones, the bolts of the doors shot back from their sockets, the massive bronze gates flew open, while the keepers fell on their faces as if struck down by the thunderbolts of Divine wrath.

The word of the Lord was upon him. He saw in his vision "the Lord our Righteousness" appear among them, he saw Him reviled and rejected, he saw Him sweat as it were great drops of blood in the garden, he saw Judas the Jew betray Him for thirty pieces of silver into the hands of a mock court, he saw Peter, one of the disciples Christ loved, raise his hands on high and swear he never knew Him, he saw Pilate call for water to wash his hands from the stains of blood that the fires of Nebuchadnezzar's furnace could not purify. He saw Him crowned with thorns, spit upon, smote in the face and nailed to the cross. He saw the spear pierce His side, he saw twelve legion of angels standing round about the cross to guard His body from further violence, for it had been written " that not a bone of Him should be broken." Then in his vision he saw Titus besiege Jerusalem, he saw the Christians of the tribe of Benjamin escape, he saw millions of the tribe of Judah and Levi slain and the remnant scattered to the four winds of heaven. He saw Israel establish a new throne, he saw them bow down to images, as Dan was wont to do in the days of Moses.

And now there passed before him a burning bunch of flax with the words, " Holy Father," " Vicar of Christ," " Head of the Church," " Infallibility." He saw this power conferred on an alien, of an alien kingdom, that God knew not of, and then he saw them bowing down to images and worshiping the queen of heaven. He saw the seven hills gain spiritual ascendency over the tribe of Dan, and then he saw the Celtic chieftains, one after another, bow down to a superior power, for the kingdom was wrenched from them and given to another. Tara must now become a heap, the same as their temple at Jerusalem. Again he saw the next empire overturned by the lion and the unicorn, and the prophecy of Ezekiel was fulfilled. And now he beholds a great wonder, for out of the loins of the lion and the unicorn there comes a great eagle with outstretched wings, that crosses the sea and plants the seed of freedom. He saw written on their banner, " we are a great people," and then he saw that it was a haven of rest for the scattered remnant of Judah and Levi. And now he sees John on the Isle of Patmos, and he hears him proclaim to the whole earth the names of the twelve tribes of the children of Israel. Where, oh where is Dan? Sunk to rise no more, for in their place he hears the name of Manasseh, "the great people," who had fulfilled the pledge, who had preached the Gospel to every nation, kindred, tongue, and people, and who were now sealed to all eternity. And now there comes to his ears the mighty blast of a trumpet, and he sees an angel with a book in his hands swear by Him that liveth forever that time shall be no longer, while angels and archangels shout " Hosanna ! "

When Jeremiah awoke he was standing in the presence of Gedaliah, who commanded that he be bound in chains and transported to Babylon, but notwithstanding the chains he seemed to be walking on air, for had not God revealed to him the beginning and the end.

As the company passed out of the city some blessed him and some cursed him. There were, however, those who said that if Zedekiah had harkened unto the voice of the prophet all would have been well. Others said he was in league with the monarch of Babylon, else why would he call that barbarian the servant of God. Others lifted up their voices in prayer and wept over Jerusalem. They knew that they were leaving their home forever. Within the walls of Babylon were the brick kilns ready for them, as the mansion of Nebuchadnezzar would not be completed in the next forty years. They knew that the foundation had been laid and that it was a journey of seven and one-half miles to walk around it. Its height, when finished with its domes and turrets, would extend up to the top of the walls. Their doom was sealed forever.

Then they fell on each other's necks and wept over

the fallen city. In this manner they reached Ramah.
The chains had galled the prophet, but he had no word
of complaint. He looked upon the tired and weary
women and children, who were chained together, and
then he wept over Jerusalem. The prophecies were as
sure to come to pass as the sun was to rise and set. As
he stood thus apart from the main body, Nebuzar Adan
approached him and handed him a document. It was
an edict from the king of Babylon, declaring him free
to go to Babylon or to return to Jerusalem.

As soon as it was noised through the city that Jeremiah had been set free, there arose a cry among the
Jews, " Traitor!" Why, if he were true to the Jews,
would Nebuchadnezzar show him any mercy? And
yet he had not only been set at liberty, but commanded
that Baruch be released from the dungeon. If this
was acceded to, then there was no doubt but that they
had been in communication during the entire siege.

Their criticisms were, however, of short duration, for
they were commanded to take up their line of march,
while Jeremiah set his face towards Jerusalem, as much
work must be accomplished before the fulfillment of the
prophecies could take place. He had seen a courier
leave Ramah, with a parchment in his hand, and ride
rapidly towards Jerusalem, but he had no thought that
the parchment was an edict setting Baruch at liberty,
and hence his surprise, when nearing the city, to meet
Baruch in company with the Ethiopian. They must

hasten now to the king's tomb, and look to the wel-
fare of Myra and Tea Tephi. Instead of entering the
gate of the city, they turned eastward and were soon going up the Mount of Olives. Turning an angle in the
path, they stopped before the mouth of the cave. It
was empty. Myra and Tea Tephi had vanished.

CHAPTER IV.

THE GOLDEN IMAGE.

BABYLON was in a blaze of glory. Jerusalem had fallen, Zedekiah, the king, was in a dungeon, while all of the gold and silver of the temple, and wherever else found, had been transported to the city. Nebuchadnezzar was now the richest man on earth, and he determined to celebrate his riches by building a golden god, ninety feet high and nine feet broad.

Babylon, at this time, was the most mighty city on earth, nor has there been a city, from that day to the present hour, that could compare with it, either in wealth, grandeur, or population. This city was founded by Nimrod one hundred and fifteen years after the Deluge, or at the same time that he founded the Assyrian Empire, whose glory extended for fourteen hundred and fifty years. Nimrod was the son of Ham, " and a mighty hunter before the Lord."

He, together with Ashur, also founded Nineveh, which was built on the east bank of the Tigris. Nineveh was eighteen and three-quarter miles long and eleven and one-quarter miles wide, being in the shape of a parallelogram. The whole circumference was sixty miles, and thus spoke the prophet Jonah, saying : " Nineveh was an exceeding great city, of three days'

(63)

journey," meaning that sixty miles was its circumference, as twenty miles was called at that time a day's
journey. The walls were one hundred feet high and
forty feet thick. There were upon the walls fifteen
hundred fortifications or towers that extended up two
hundred feet, making the whole elevation at these
points three hundred feet.

Babylon was built on a plain, and was exactly square,
each square being fifteen miles long. The walls were
three hundred and fifty feet high and eighty-seven feet
thick, enclosing a surface of sixty miles. These walls
were built of brick, and surrounded by a deep ditch
filled with water, and as the earth was dug from the
ditch that made the brick, some conception of the
depth and breadth of it can be gained by considering
the height and thickness of the walls. Moreover, the
earth came from the same ditch that made the tower
of Babel, which was one-half mile in circumference and
one-eighth of a mile high.

On each square of the city walls were twenty-five
brazen gates, that in times of peace were kept open
through the day and closed at sunset every night. A
branch of the river Euphrates ran directly through the
city from north to south, having a wall on either side.
In the centre of the city was a massive bridge that
crossed the river to the old palace on the east, and this
was connected with the new palace on the west by an
arched passageway running under the river.

The old palace, founded and built by Nimrod, was three and three-quarter miles in circumference, while the new one, built by Nebuchadnezzar, was seven and one-half miles in circumference. The walls, or hanging towers, one of the seven wonders of the world, were in the form of a square, each side being four hundred feet, and were carried up by terraces, one above another, to a height of three hundred and fifty feet. This was resting on massive arches of masonry. There were on the top of the hanging towers engines of curious workmanship used for drawing water to irrigate the mighty trees and shrubs that grew on each terrace. The Tower of Babel was built on the east side of the river by the side of the old palace, and was filled with temples of great magnificence for the worship of the golden god Belus. The amount of gold and silver dedicated to Belus was estimated at $105,000,000. A sloping roadway ran to the top in a circular form on the outside of the tower, so that a horseman could drive to the summit as easily as he could drive around the city. The foundations were laid, and the plans drawn, for the tower to be exactly one-half mile in circumference and one-half mile high ; but after carrying it up forty rods their language was confounded, and they were scattered throughout the earth. The population in the days of Nebuchadnezzar is variously estimated at from ten to twenty millions.

The gold that was pillaged from the temple at Jerusalem was now placed in the hands of the sculptor, and behold a mammoth god had risen up in the plains of Dura and surplanted the God of the Hebrews. Then a herald cried aloud, saying, " When ye hear the sound of all kinds of music, fall down and worship the golden image that Nebuchadnezzar has set up." " And whosoever falleth not down and worshipeth shall the same hour be cast into the midst of a burning fiery furnace."

The sound of revelry began. The trumpet sounded over the plain, the cornet, the flute, the harp, and hundreds of other instruments rang out on the morning air, and every Chaldean bowed his face to the ground and worshiped. But the Jews, where were they?

Notwithstanding their captivity, their thoughts were centered on Jerusalem and the temple erected to the Most High God. Never would they blaspheme their God by bowing the knee to a graven image. The commandments given to their fathers were as sacred now as they were when Moses received them from the Most High God on the Mount.

When the king learned that his captive slaves ignored his command he was in a towering passion. He called them before him, and thus he spake : " You are my slaves. Who are you, that thus lift up your voices against my majesty and power? You shall bow down and worship my god, or you shall be cast into the furnace. Now, obey." The Jews looked up at the monarch, and then their thoughts went back over

the past history of their people. Did not God deliver
Isaac on Mount Moriah? Did He not deliver David
from the hands of Goliath? Did He not deliver Samson from the hands of the Philistines? "No, a thousand times no!" Rather the furnace here than hereafter.

"Will you bow?" cried the king.

"Never!"

"Then, by heavens, ye die. What ho! the furnace!
Bind these slaves, and who is the God that shall deliver
them out of my hands?"

The three Jews were seized by six stalwart Chaldeans and thrown, bound hand and foot, into the furnace. And when the king looked, behold, the six men
had fallen dead before the furnace, and were being
consumed by the intense heat. Seeing the men on fire
in front of the furnace, he stooped down and looked in,
when he sprang back as though stung by a scorpion.
Trembling with excitement, he cried out, "Did not we
throw three men, bound, into the furnace?" "True,
O king." "Lo, I see four men loose walking in the
fire, and the form of the fourth is like the Son of God.
Shadrach, Meshach, Abednego, come forth, and whosoever hereafter sayeth anything against your God shall
be cut in pieces and their houses shall be made a dung-
hill."

The miracle that Nebuchadnezzar saw had the same
effect upon him that the death of a loved one has upon

us. It softens our nature; it sweetens our temper; it humbles our pride; it brings us nearer the throne. But, alas! how soon we forget the chastening rod; how soon the tears are dried up; how soon we forget God. In the history of every individual there come up before them scenes and incidents in their lives, that are stereotyped on their memory to such an extent that they are satisfied they have witnessed the same thing before, and yet they know it is simply a matter of impossibility. Where then did they receive the impression?

To a large number of people this has led to a firm belief that they have lived before and passed through those same scenes, and yet investigation demonstrates the fact that the impression received at the time is the result of a dream. A dream that it would take an hour to relate will flash through the brain in the twinkling of an eye; and while we may not be able to recall one word of it, nevertheless it has left its impression for all time, and can never be thoroughly effaced from the memory. This is a personal identity which is always with us, and this was what led Nebuchadnezzar to feel that he had dreamed a marvelous dream, that had faded away so effectually that there was only left within him his own personal identity. This feeling is joyful or sorrowful, according to the state of the mind or the physical condition of the body. To Nebuchadnezzar it had left an impression of coming evil, and he was anxious

FORM OF THE ARK OF THE COVENANT.

to know, not only the dream, but the interpretation
thereof. If he had walked out to the plains of Dura,
and beheld for the first time the golden image he had
set up, he would in all probability have said within
himself, " I have seen this same thing before, but
where ?" And this would have led to a train of
thought, " Have I not lived before ? "

Isaiah says : " For behold, I create new heavens and
a new earth, and the former shall not be remembered
nor come into mind."

There was implanted in Daniel a latent psychological
element that prayer developed into inspiration, and inspiration into power. In fact, the mind of Daniel was
so thoroughly imbued with the spirit and understanding of the will of God, that he becomes to us a living
monument of the truth of prophecy, and thus he re-
veals to the king his dream of the great image, and that
the little stone cut out of the mountain without hands
that smote the image would become a great mountain
and fill the whole world. " And it shall stand forever."

Again, the king had a marvelous dream, and this
time the impression was so deep that he could relate
every word of it. Trembling with fear, he called Daniel
and from him received his sentence. " They shall
drive thee from men, and thy dwelling shall be with
the beasts of the field ; and they shall make thee to
eat grass as oxen, and they shall wet thee with the
dews of heaven, and seven times shall pass over thee

till thou know that the Most High ruleth." One year
has passed away, and the king has forgotten every
promise. Daniel is in trouble; for well he knows that
the king, when not puffed up with pride, has more
native wisdom than any king who has ever ruled over
Babylon. He knows that Jeremiah loves and respects
him, and has called him the servant of God. But, alas !
the hour has come. The king walks forth, and, smiting
his chest, says: "Is not this great Babylon that I have
built, for the house of the kingdom, by the might of
my power, and for the honor of my majesty." And
while he yet spake there came a voice from heaven,
saying, "O king Nebuchadnezzar, thy kingdom has
departed from thee." "And in that same hour he was
driven out, and did eat grass like the oxen, and his
body was wet with the dews of heaven till his hairs were
grown like eagles' feathers, and his nails like birds'
claws." The prophecy was fulfilled, and Judah's God
vindicated.

CHAPTER V.

EOCHAID.

STANDING on the deck of the ship *Hermon*, which had just entered the harbor of Joppa, laden with tin from the north of Ireland, stood Eochaid, the Prince of Wales. This ship was owned and manned by the tribe of Dan, who had settled in Ireland during the reign of King Solomon, and had carried with them the secret signs and passwords of the Mystic Brotherhood. Already there were thousands of the tribe of Dan living in Ulster under the name of Danauns. The youth, for he was not past two-and-twenty, bore the *insignia* of a " Knight of the East." He had been knighted by his father, Hermon, the monarch of England, Scotland, Ireland and Wales, prior to his departure to the Orient. The knight was taller than the average youth, with a contour that would meet all the requirements of a poet or sculptor. His muscles were hard and thoroughly developed, through training in a school of physical culture; his shoulders were broad, his chest deep, his movements agile; and woe betide him who put his prowess to the test, either in heraldry or swordsmanship. The youth stood long and thoughtfully gazing at this ancient and historic city and harbor. Here it

(73)

was that the cedars, which had been so cunningly fashioned, were floated down for the building of the holy temple at Jerusalem.   Here it was that classical mythology had chained Andromeda to the rock to be devoured by the sea-monster.   Here was a city, ancient even at that early period. Joppa, which by interpretation means beauty, was situated on the shore of the Mediterranean Sea, thirty-three miles from Jerusalem. The city was the dividing line between Dan and Ephraim, each owning fifty miles of coast.   The youth had heard much of the magnificence of King Solomon's temple and of the visit of the Queen of Sheba, and he wondered if its glory were wrought through the skill of man alone, or was he under the inspiration of the Hebrew God.

Why did Dan leave this beautiful climate, where the orange and the date grow, to live on the ice-bound coast of the Atlantic Ocean? He had read that it was in fulfillment of prophecy; but if this were so, why did they cast the prophets into dungeons? Could they expect foreign nations to believe in a God that they themselves repudiated? While Moses was thundering on the mount, Dan was worshiping calves on the plain. Was not the power that Moses possessed the power of mind over matter, of reason over superstition, of education over ignorance, of light over darkness? And yet, why am I here? why was I given a power of conception, reason, and understanding to lead my thoughts toward

another life, if "death ends all"? To what avail was the
magnificent temple of King Solomon's wisdom, if fifty-
eight short years buried it forever? "Ah, the more I
think the more mystified I become, and yet I know
that this grand design had an author; I know that the
first man had a Maker; I know that the grand laws
that govern our system, and move all suns and worlds
harmoniously, had a Creator, and that Creator has
power to create in us a new life, to continue on when
time shall be no longer. Oh, there must be a God in
Israel, even though He suffers them to worship idols
and persecute the saints. My soul revolts at the idea
of an eternal sleep. No, no; God never created man
without a design as to his future state. He lives again,
the essence of divinity, and will go on, his soul expand-
ing, his conceptions and aspirations reaching out toward
a perfect day. Onward he goes, rising higher and
higher, nobler and nobler; yea, grander and grander,
until he becomes the personification of God Himself,
else why was he endowed with those principles and with
that temple of thought and perception to examine into
all the laws of God? He weighs the planets as in the
balances; he determines eclipses; he fathoms the principles and the laws. The question, ' If a man die, shall
he live again?' would never have been asked if there
had not been created within him hopes and expectations
that would go on to a realization of immortality. The
essence of divinity within us will diffuse itself through-

out all eternity, like a grain of musk, that diffuses its
aroma throughout every corner of the house for thousands of years, and yet it has lost nothing. The same
grain of musk remains, and must remain, to all eternity.
Not one particle of matter can ever be destroyed, and
hence not one soul can ever escape from its eternal en-
vironments.

" Oh, I must see Jeremiah ; he knows all the mys-
teries of immortality. And yet, why is he and Daniel
and Ezekiel in captivity? Is it because their prophecies are false? We will wait and see. Jeremiah has
prophesied that Jerusalem will fall, the temple will be
burned, and that Zedekiah will be carried in chains
captive into Babylon. If these things take place, then
Lord, I believe. ' Hark!' what mean those shouts
from the walls of Joppa, and why are they swarming
on the housetops, with their faces toward Jerusalem?"

Turning his eyes in that direction, he saw a pillar of
fire ascending up toward heaven, and then he heard a cry
that rang in his ears until his soul fainted within him,
" Jerusalem has fallen! "

Fear, mingled with rage, had now taken possession
of the people. To what extent would the victorious
monarch carry on his work of devastation and ruin?
They saw now only the bondage of their fathers before
them. They saw the city overthrown, their brethren
cut down out of time, and their king in chains. For
the first time the prophecies of Jeremiah rang in their

ears, and now they were fulfilled. " Go ye up upon her
walls, but make not a full end. Take away her battlements, for they are not the Lord's. For the house of
Israel, and the house of Judah, have dealt very treach-
erously against me, saith the Lord." The prophecies
were fulfilled, but the end was not yet. Slavery for
their wives and little ones ; the yoke and the halter for
themselves.

Girding on his armor, the youth stood as one chained
to the spot. Was it not in fulfillment of some prophecy that brought him from his island home to draw his
sword in defense of a fallen race? Long and sorrow-
fully he gazed toward Jerusalem ; hopes blasted, anti-
cipations wrecked, joys banished, fears aroused. Where
should he go? At last the sun, which had been transformed into an ocean of blood, sank into the sea ; the
beacon fires were kindled, the blood-red moon came up
over the Mount of Olives, the groans and sobs one
after another died away, midnight came, and Joppa
slept.

Thirty days had now passed, when early in the morning, before the sun had yet risen, a stalwart Ethiopian
rode up to the palace in Joppa, leading a powerful
black stallion. The slave bore letters from the governor of Jerusalem to the occidental prince, extending to
him the hospitalities of the city of Mizpah. Nebuchadnezzar had learned that the prince had been invited by
Zedekiah to visit Palestine, and he had no desire to im-

pose upon him any suffering or inconvenience. He knew that Hermon was the most powerful monarch of the west, with a mighty navy at his command, and hence he bade Gedeliah send a messenger to Joppa to meet the prince and to conduct him safely into the city. The prince received the letters and then turned his attention toward the Ethiopian. He had never seen a more powerfully built man. Standing some six feet seven inches tall, with a breadth of shoulders and a girth of chest that would have put Hercules to flight. Could he be trusted? If so, they could cut their way through any army of men. If the Ethiopian became his friend he had nothing to fear.

The sun had just risen when the two men mounted their horses, and were soon on their way to Lydda.

"Why so sorrowful?"

The Ethiopian looked·at the speaker, and as their eyes met there passed through each of them a feeling of trust and confidence.

"You are a Knight of the East?

"I am."

"And I can trust you?"

"To the ends of the earth."

Thus from that moment there sprang up between king and slave a friendship that was cemented for all time.

"My master," said the slave, "is Jeremiah. He is, like yourself, a Knight of the East. When Jerusalem

was taken, he was liberated by the order of Nebuchadnezzar, while my former master, the king, was carried
away captive. The two princess, Myra and Tea
Tephi, were found by me in the palace garden ; they
not knowing at the time that the family had escaped
through the passage toward Jericho. I took them to
the king's tomb, as that was a favorite place of Jeremiah's when at liberty. I knew that they must be hidden from the Chaldeans, as they had sworn to slay every
member of the king's family. When Jeremiah returned
that night from Ramah, we, in company with Baruch,
went to the tomb, and, lo, they had been stolen away.
My heart sank within me, for I was afraid of the
prophet. But he took me by the hand and comforted
me, saying 'I was a servant of the Most High God,
and a slave no longer.' "

"And is that what makes you sad?" asked the prince.

"No. The princess are stolen away and I fear me
some evil will befall them. Oh, if you could only see
Tea Tephi. God never fashioned a more beautiful
piece of clay. I loved her from a child as I can never
love my own, and all night long on my way to Joppa I
smote my breast and cried, 'Alas! alas! for human
idolatry.' "

"Is Jeremiah a true prophet?" asked the prince.

"Yes, he is one of God's anointed, and while the
Jews cry out against him he would lay down his life to
save them; but you know that he floats down in the tide

of God's truths, and that makes it easy for him. The Jews try to stem the current of God's displeasure and hence fail. Jeremiah knows the way and follows the truth. While it was just as hard for him to see our beautiful temple destroyed as it was for the king, he had no power to save. He had only the gift of knowledge, while Zedekiah was steeped in ignorance. Now he is reaping the whirlwind of his own election."

"If God told Jeremiah that the city would be overthrown and the temple burned, and he had loved them with the same love that Zedekiah possessed, why did he not save them?" asked the prince.

"Because his power was limited. If you do wrong, is there not always a still small voice within you that pleads for the right just the same as though a prophet of the Lord had spoken to you?"

"Yes."

"Then if you do wrong, you see, the still small voice is limited in its power, just the same as though you had been spoken to by the prophet. Jeremiah pleaded with the king, just the same as God pleads with us. Some obey and are saved, others disobey and are lost."

"Do you believe that God punishes hereafter?"

"No."

"Then why do you say some are lost? Did Jeremiah punish the king?"

"No."

"Was not Jeremiah's mission to save?"

"Yes."

"Then who punished the king?'

"Why, I suppose it was through his disobedience, in not obeying the voice of the prophet." Then said the Ethiopian, "He elected to be overthrown. Just the same way with man and his God. God does not punish, He saves. Man, if he is lost, is lost through his own election."

"Do you believe the word of God to be perfect?" asked the prince.

"It was when given to man, but became imperfect."

"Why?"

"Because whatever man touches becomes at once contaminated."

"Are you a pupil of Jeremiah?"

"I have learned much of him that used to be dark and foreboding. I could not see just why God punished a whole city for the sins of a few people, but through the teaching of the prophet those things have been made clear."

"How?"

"Because if the prophet should cry aloud in the streets of Jerusalem, 'Yet forty days and the city shall be destroyed if you do not clean your sewers and filter your water that is full of deadly germs,' I say that if within forty days they did not do it and were destroyed by black death and cholera, the people elected it and consequently punished themselves. Thousands die every year on their pilgrimage to the temple to worship, and it has been noted that they who are clean are usually free from disease and death. It is the unclean who die of the plague and the leprosy, but their touch contaminates the clean, for if we associate with the leper we become leprous; if we associate with the wine-bibbers we become drunkards; and thus the plague came to Jerusalem, not because it was the will of God, but because we were shut up without the facilities of purifying ourselves or burying our dead. The city was not cursed by God, but by its rulers."

The prince became thoughtful. He had learned more from this humble follower of Jeremiah than he ever had at the colleges of Lothair Crofin. If the Ethiopian explained so lucidly, what a fountain of knowledge there must be in the brain of the prophet.

As the two gained the brow of the hill that looked down into Mizpah they were met by a sight that caused them to start back and draw rein. Ishmael was just .leaving with a large body of men, together with the captives of the city. The Ethiopian recognized Jeremiah and Baruch, together with the king's daughters.

As soon as they had passed out of sight on their way to the Ammonites, they rode down to the city and gave the alarm.

CHAPTER VI.

ISHMAEL.

WHEN Nebuchadnezzar had carried away all of the noble families of Jerusalem he made Gedaliah governor over the poor families and all those who had escaped out of the city after the siege. Gedaliah was a righteous man, and consequently when the Jews heard that he had been appointed governor they hastened back to the city. Among those who escaped during the siege was Ishmael, one of the king's sons, a captain of the guard, who was the most wicked and crafty man in all Jerusalem, and as a matter of fact the only coward who deserted his post. As soon as the plague entered the city he went out to Baalis, the king of the Ammonites, to await events. That Jerusalem must fall he had no doubt, as the prophet had foretold that all going out of the city would be saved alive and all who remained would fall by either the sword, pestilence, or famine. If he was a true prophet, then all of his father's family would be swept out of time, and he would be the seed royal of the throne of David. He would accept Jeremiah's prophecies as true and escape. If the family were all slain, then he would return to Jerusalem and assert his power. It had been prophesied that the throne should have an heir until Shiloh came, but Jeremiah had said that this heir would not occupy the throne at Jerusalem over the Jews, but the throne over the Israelites. The Israelites were lost, but the prophecies concerning them were that Shiloh's mission on earth was to them and them alone, and that their throne should be established with the seed royal of the house of David as their leader. Who then would be left save himself to become their king?

As soon as he heard that the city had fallen and that his father's family were all slain he believed the words of the prophet, and taking ten men with him entered Mizpah. Already Gedaliah had been appointed governor, and was ready to meet the king's son and deal honorably with him. He had been warned by Johanan that Ishmael was a wicked and crafty prince, and the only way to make a good prince of him was to kill him, but the governor would not listen to any such proposal. He believed that by entertaining him as became the seed of the house of David he could secure his friendship, and thereby make him a firm ally. When Ishmael arrived he was met as a king. The house had been set in order, and the banquet hall rang out with the sound of music. Wine flowed like a river. Jests were passed to and fro between governor and prince, until Gedaliah began to be overcome. Then Ishmael rose up and slew him, together with all who were in the house.

Night came on, and as soon as the shadows cast

their mantle over the city they went into the streets
and slew all the Jews and all of the soldiers left there
by Nebuchadnezzar to guard the city. Early in the
morning there came eighty Jews, bearing presents to
Gedaliah. They were invited into the court and all
slain save a few who had more treasures hid in the field.
The pit of Asa was now reeking with the blood and
bodies of the slain. Not less than one thousand Jews
and Chaldean soldiers had perished during the night.
In the morning he sent out spies to bring in any found
in the mountains, and it was by one of these spies that
the tomb was discovered and the king's daughters
brought into Mizpah.

When he saw his sisters he disbelieved the words of
the prophet and ordered that Jeremiah and Baruch be
found and brought before him. Jeremiah was a false
prophet and he should pay the penalty. Myra and
Tea Tephi should die. Who were they, to stand before him and the throne of Israel? As soon as they
were found they were brought before Ishmael, and a
council declared that there should no mercy be shown
to either of them, consequently the prophet and
Baruch were bound in chains to Myra and Tea Tephi,
and again they took up the line of march towards the
country of Ammon, where death would be meted out
to them in the most horrible manner.

As they were going out of the city they were recognized by the Ethiopian. The alarm was given, and

soon all the country round about Jerusalem were has-
tening toward Mizpah.

They had escaped the war, the famine, and the pestilence only to meet a death more foul at the hands of
an assassin. "To arms! to arms! and wipe out this
foul blot." Johanan, a mighty man of valor, had soon
collected an army of men, among whom were the
prince and the slave. The Jews were bowed down with
sorrow, as they knew that under the good government
of Gedaliah peace would quickly have been restored.
Now they were eager for the combat. The sun was
well past the meridian when Johanan gave the command to march. The cavalry had been divided into
two companies, one under Johanan and the other under
Jezaniah. As the cavalry went out of Mizpah and
took the road south leading down to Hebron, a prolonged shout rent the air. "Onward to victory!"
"Death to the traitor!" Toward sunset they came to
the plains of Hebron and saw Ishmael and his company
encamped at the fountain. They had been seen by
Ishmael, and now there seemed to be hurried work
going on in his camp.

The Ethiopian sat on his horse like one in a dream,
for he saw the chains loosed from the princess, while
two powerful men seized them, and springing into the
saddle shot away over the plains. The prince saw the
movements, and, like a flash of lightning, the two men
dashed away after them.

When Ishmael saw the prince and the Ethiopian ride
away after the two men who bore the princess, he hurriedly gave orders, and in a moment twelve men had
mounted and rode to the rescue. The horses that the
prince and the slave rode were more powerful and fleet
than any that Ishmael possessed, hence only a few moments expired before the prince rode up to the one
who bore Tea Tephi and, drawing his sword, he cleft
him from crown to chin. In the meantime the Ethiopian had borne down on the rider who carried Myra,
and, throwing his javelin, it passed directly through the
neck of the horse. He stopped short, threw up his
head, and fell headlong to the earth. Before he had
reached the ground the slave threw himself from his
horse, and before the Ammonite could recover he was
borne down to the earth, while Myra was seized in
the Ethiopian's powerful grasp and borne to a place of
safety; then springing into his saddle he turned to face
the enemy, and he was not a moment too soon. A
powerful blow had been aimed at him by the leader of
the gang, which was parried by the sword of the prince,
and before the Ammonite could recover, his head was
severed from his body.

It was then that the people from both camps watched
the battle with intense excitement. Never had either
Ishmael or Johanan witnessed such a combat. While
the Ethiopian bore them down by his ponderous weight
and power, the prince like a lightning flash mowed them

down before him like grain before the reaper. Never before had such a knight been seen on the plains of Gibeon. Who was he, and from whence came his superior knowledge in the art of swordsmanship? Could the twelve men retake the princess? " No, by heavens, they are conquered ! " cried Ishmael, as the wily Irishman parried a thrust aimed at his horse ; then shouting to the Ethiopian, " Now, by the rock of Kilkenny, let us finish these barbarians ! " he cleft the leader in twain. Then spurring his horse up to the side of the slave, who was engaged in warding off the last three, he arose in the saddle, and in a moment the victory was theirs. The last man had bit the dust. And now there went up a shout from the camp of Johanan, " Death to the assassin ! "

While this combat had been taking place the captive Jews had gone over to Johanan, and they were being armed preparatory to meeting the company of Ishmael. Ishmael had been weakened by the death of fourteen men, and this had reduced his valiant men of war. He had been reinforced at the fountain of Hebron, but he feared the prince and the slave. If Johanan were alone he would meet him in equal combat, and he was assured that he could conquer, but now he must take to flight. Mounting his horse, he together with eight men made their escape.

When Jeremiah saw the prince his heart leaped within him. He had seen him before, but where ?

Every movement was stereotyped in his memory.
His face, his voice, all were as familiar to him as the
face and voice of Baruch, and yet he could not recall
his name. Bowing his head, his mind went out over
the past. At last he sprang to his feet and, seizing
Baruch by the arm, he cried, " 'Tis he, 'tis he of whom
I spake. I have seen him a thousand times in my
dreams! He will save Israel, and establish the new
throne."

When the prince rode up with Tea Tephi in his
arms, the prophet raised his hands and commanded
the blessing of God to rest upon them. Already the
hearts of both were in each other's keeping, yet they
knew it not. The prince sprang from his horse, giving
the princess into the keeping of Johanan ; then bowing
down before the prophet and kissing the hem of his
garment, he asked his blessing. The prophet laid his
hand on the head of the prince, then raising his eyes
toward Heaven, he prayed that the Lord would give
him a sign, whereby he might know that from the
loins of the prince he blessed the house of Israel would
be established. And now there comes the rolling of a
distant thunder. Gradually it comes on, until the whole
heavens have been transformed into a mighty host of
horses and chariots of fire. The thundering of the
artillery ceased, and from the battlements of Heaven
there came a voice, saying : " Through his throne
Israel shall be saved. Know ye not that God made a

covenant with David, by a pinch of salt, that the seed
of Judah should rule over Israel forever?"

When the morning came the command was given to
move on to Chimham, which is at the entrance going
down into Egypt. A dissension had arisen between
the prophet and the people. Johanan was afraid of
the Chaldeans, in that Gedaliah had been slain. He
had before agreed to accept the word of the Lord
through the prophet, but now he was rebellious, and
would force the people to go into Egypt. Again they
asked Jeremiah to inquire of the Lord, and again the
word of the Lord came unto him, saying: "If you will
abide in land, I will build you up and not pull you
down, for I repent me of the evil I have done unto you.
Be not afraid of the King of Babylon, for I am with
you. But if ye say, I will go into the land of Egypt,
then it shall come to pass that the sword you fear shall
overtake you, and the famine whereof you are afraid
shall follow you there in Egypt, that ye die. For thus
saith the Lord of Hosts, the God of Israel. As mine
anger and my fury has been poured forth upon the
inhabitants of Jerusalem, so shall my fury be poured
forth on you when ye shall enter Egypt." "Then,"
said Azariah, "thou speakest falsely. God hath not
sent thee to say, go not into Egypt; but Baruch set-
teth thee on against us to deliver us into the hands of
the Chaldeans." So there was a division, for neither
Johanan nor Azariah would listen to the voice of the

prophet, "but commanded all, both Jeremiah, and Baruch, and the king's daughters, and all of the people to pass over into Egypt."

When the prince had heard all the words of the prophet and of the captains he was exceedingly sorry, as he believed the words of Jeremiah, and was satisfied that no good thing could come out of Egypt. The prince had come to love Jeremiah as one of God's anointed, and he hearkened unto him. Jeremiah had warned the prince, as soon as they had crossed over into Egypt, to take the princess by stealth and go back to Jerusalem. God had shown him that they were all safe from the hands of the King of Babylon, as he was then preparing to make war on the Moabites and the Ammonites, and he certainly would despoil Egypt. As soon as possible he, with Baruch, would make their escape and meet him in Jerusalem. He had informed him of the whereabouts of the king's tomb, and should any trouble occur to secrete the princess. The prophet knew the prince to be a Knight of the East, and he had no hesitancy in placing the princess in his keeping. Accordingly, at midnight, on the day they arrived in Egypt, the prince and the Ethiopian were in the saddle. Two horses were secured from the company, while cautiously the princess mounted, and when the morning came they were well on their way toward Jerusalem.

CHAPTER VII.

EGYPT.

EGYPT is bounded on the north by the Mediterranean, on the south by Ethiopia, on the east by the Red Sea and the Isthmus of Suez, and on the west by Libya. The Nile runs from south to north through the whole country, a distance of six hundred miles. The distance from Jerusalem to Memphis (the capital city of the Pharoahs in the days of Joseph) was two hundred and seventy miles. The distance from Hebron, in the land of Canaan (twenty miles south of Jerusalem), was two hundred and fifty miles, although it was only forty miles from Hebron to the entrance into Egypt.

The land of Canaan must not be confounded with Cana of Galilee, as that was eighty miles north of Hebron. These two places are frequently confounded by commentators, as is Zechariah the prophet, who was slain between the temple and the altar, with Zachariah the son of Baruch, who was slain in the temple. Babylon lay nearly due east, five hundred miles from Jerulem, across the northern part of the Arabian desert. Mesopotamia was one hundred and fifty miles north of

Palestine. To the south lay the country of the Am-
monities and the Moabites.

Menes, or Mizraim, the first king and founder of the
Egyptian Empire, was a son of Ham. He, together with
Nimrod his nephew, a grandson of Ham, founded Babylon, and were the chief promoters of the building of
the Tower of Babel ; but after the languages were confounded Ham went down into Egypt and laid the
foundation of Memphis. His son Menes became the first
king, and founded Thebes, which 1,500 years B.C. became the capital city, having supplanted Memphis, the
home of Joseph and the birth-place of Ephraim and
Manasseh. Directly in front of the city lay the great
Necropolis, in the centre of which towered the pyramids. At this time the great pyramid was eight hundred feet square at its base and eight hundred feet
high. Thirty years was occupied in building it, with a
force of one hundred thousand men. Job, a profound
astronomer, is supposed to have been the chief architect. He was a grandson of Jacob and a contemporary
with Moses.

At the time of the seventy years' captivity, Thebes
was the capital city. This was one of the most beautiful cities on earth. " In the grand palace was a hall
329 feet long and 170 feet wide, supported by 12 massive columns of solid granite, 60 feet high and 36 feet
in circumference, while these were surrounded by 122
columns, 49 feet high and 27 feet in circumference.

Directly in front of the palace were two obelisks, 92 feet high and 8 feet square at the base. It was surrounded by a mighty wall, containing 100 brazen gates, from which in time of war 20,000 war chariots could be sent out, and 10,000 men from each gate." This city was located on the river Nile, in Upper Egypt. "Their religion was the worship of Osiris and Isis, which represented the sun and moon, together with the ox, dog, cat, wolf, hawk, crocodile, ibis, and ape. They were probably the most superstitious people that ever lived on the face of the earth. While the Hebrews sojourned in Goshen they partook largely of these superstitions, and hence we find Dan setting up a golden calf at the foot of Mount Sinai."

From the remotest antiquity the year has been 365 days, 6 hours. The river Nile overflows and waters the whole country, as it seldom rains in Egypt. The height of its rising is 24 feet. If less, then there is a famine in the land. The inhabitants begin to sow in October and November, and reap in March and April. On the 1st of June a strong northeasterly wind begins to blow, which continues for four months, and this keeps the water back, which otherwise would flow off too fast, and thereby produce famine. This is one of the strong links in the chain of Supreme Control. The law differs in Palestine, as there fixed rains fall on the country twice a year.

At this time there were in Egypt 2,000 cities and

towns, in which were magnificent temples erected to a
thousand-and-one gods, but none to the worship of the
true God. Written on the sarcophagus of one of the
dead rulers, in the temple of Isis, is this inscription, " I
am whatever has been, and is, and shall be, and no
mortal hath yet pierced the veil that shrouds me."
Thus we find the children of Noah, whom God loved
and saved from destruction, peopled throughout the
earth. Shem, from the Euphrates to the Indian Ocean,
including the Assyrians, Persians, Chaldeans, and
Lydians. They were also the founders and builders of
Damascus.

Japhet was scattered through Europe and Asia.
They were the founders of Media, Cappadocia, Tarsus,
Cyprus, even unto Cadiz.

The posterity of Ham were in Africa and in the land
of Canaan. You must remember that Noah did not
curse Ham, but Canaan. "And he said, cursed be
Canaan; a servant of servants shall he be unto his
brethren. And he said, blessed be the Lord God of
Shem." From Shem came Abraham, and through his
seed the final overthrow of Canaan, of whom were the
Philistines, Jebusites, Ammonites, Hivites, and dozens
of other tribes equally as bad. From the remnant
came the Moors and Arabs, together with the Ethio-
pians and the Egyptians. These entire nations were
void of every element that pertains to the worship of
Jehovah, Nimrod being the first to turn the people

toward the worship of idols; hence the wisdom of God in calling Abraham up out of Chaldea to become the leader of a people who would keep in remembrance the true source of all things. By remembering this, we can understand just why God spake through the prophets to this peculiar people, as they, and they alone, were to establish the two kingdoms that would have their full fruition in the evangelization of the whole world. Noah, through faith, blessed Abraham; Abraham, through faith, the nations of the earth.

When Jeremiah awoke the next morning he was in sore distress, for well he knew that not one soul who had crossed over into Egypt would ever return save those who heard and believed; and who out of that vast number believed? Not one, save Baruch and himself. Then the word of the Lord came to him, and said: "For I will punish them that dwell in the land of Egypt, as I have punished Jerusalem, by the sword, by the famine, and by the pestilence. Behold I will watch over them for evil, and not for good; and all the men of Judah that are in the land of Egypt shall be consumed by the sword, and by the famine, until there shall be an end of them. And this shall be a sign unto you, saith the Lord, that *I will punish you in this place*, that ye may know that my words will surely stand against you for evil."

Already a famine threatened them. The vast multitude of people had consumed most that had been

brought from Mizpah, while the Egyptians shunned
them, as they were an abomination unto them. Never
had an Egyptian associated with a Jew since the days
of Joseph, and now they refused to sell their corn except at the most extravagant prices. Pestilence broke
out through the want of proper nourishment, and death
claimed them by the scores every day; and yet they
refused to return into the land of their fathers. In the
camp of Azariah a plot was being formulated for the
destruction of the prophet. His presence among them
was more grievous than Moses in Egypt.

In the fields of Egypt there is a small poisonous serpent, known as the asp, whose sting is as deadly as
death itself. They had already secured one, and now
awaited the time when Jeremiah slept to release the
serpent in his tent. Should that fail, then they would
cut him down with the sword. Evening came on, and
the prophet retired to his tent, but not to sleep. The
ways of God were, as ever, a mystery to him, but he had
never questioned their justice. Now women and children were dying by the scores and hundreds, and there
was none to deliver. Why had God brought all these
punishments, simply because they had crossed the line
into Egypt? And yet they had disobeyed, in exactly
the same way that Adam and Eve had disobeyed, and
death would be meeted out to them. Moses disobeyed,
and was not permitted to enter into the promised land.
Zedekiah had disobeyed, and all Jerusalem was in

mourning. Johanan and Azariah had disobeyed, and death would be their portion, because God had decreed it. Sin entered the world, and death through the sin of disobedience.

At this moment he became aware of the presence of another beside themselves in the tent. Who was he, and why so much stealth? Baruch was sleeping in his cot, on the other side of the tent, little dreaming of the danger that threatened them, for the Seer was sure evil was about to befall them. While straining every nerve to catch the faintest sound, he hears the hiss of a serpent; then he knows his doom is sealed, unless God is with him. He had never doubted the wisdom and benevolence of God toward those who walk in His footsteps, and he would rely on His promises even though he were slain. Silently the murderer glides up to the couch of the Seer and, stooping over him, listens. The prophet feels his breath on his face, but he makes no movement; nothing but the heavy breathing of the supposed sleepers is heard in the tent. The mantle that covers the prophet is then gently raised, the box containing the serpent is placed beside him, the cover is quickly removed, the mantle dropped into its place, and the man glides from the tent.

As soon as the assassin was gone Baruch arose and struck the flint. A spark rested on the punk, which was soon fanned into a flame, and from that he lit the torch; then, carefully raising the mantle, he saw that the asp had not moved. Taking up the cover, he placed it over the box and quickly left the tent. Not one word had been spoken by either. Did Baruch think the prophet was asleep? Hour after hour passed away, and still he came not. Where was he? Surely he would not allow the serpent to do him an injury?

When Baruch had awoke and heard the hiss of the serpent, he knew that death lurked within the folds of tent. He had overheard the threats made against the life of the Seer, and now the hour had come when they would take their revenge upon him in a most cowardly and dastardly manner. He had faith to believe that God would protect him from the fangs of the serpent, but how?

As soon as the man was gone, he was on his feet, and taking the box from the cot he hurriedly left the tent and sought the tent of the assassin. Nor did he have far to go, for he was satisfied that the work was that of Azariah, or the tools that were under his command. While he was thus standing in a listening attitude, a hand was gently laid upon his shoulder, and a voice whispered in his ear, "Give me the box, and get thee gone, for thy life, as well that of the Seer, is in danger." "But as for me also, mine eye shall not spare, neither will I have pity, but I will recompense their way upon their head."

Early in the morning, even before it was yet day, a cry ran through the camp. "A new plague; a new plague!" Heman and Eliezer are both dead, and it certainly must be the work of Jeremiah. Azariah hated both the prophet and Baruch with an intense hatred, but had stood in fear of the Jews. Now the time had come when he could have revenge upon them, backed up by the people, and so he took up the shout, "Death to the traitors!" A council was called, and it was unanimously decided that they should die on that very hour. Accordingly Johanan and Azariah commanded that they be summoned from the tent to meet their doom. The tent was empty. At that moment Jeremiah and Baruch were sitting under the great oak of Abraham, which is at the fountain of Hebron.

CHAPTER VIII.

THE ARK OF THE COVENANT.

AT the northeast corner of the ruins of the temple at Jerusalem two men were engaged in earnest conversation. To a casual observer they were as two who had just met and were exchanging friendly salutations, but the business on hand with them was of a more weighty and momentous character.

Standing just within the shadow of a fallen pillar were seven Fellow Crafts. Receiving a sign from Baruch, the men advanced, giving the password, due guard, and grand sign; then producing a strong cord they proceeded to lower one of their fellows into the opening that had been made, preparatory to the final act of bringing to light the sacred corner-stone.

"You will know it by the iron ring in the corner," said Jeremiah, speaking to the fellow who was descending. "It lays just over the vaults, wherein is the ark of the covenant and the tables of the law. Be careful, as the heat methinks has slivered and peradventure cracked it. This is Bethel. None other than the house of God. This is Jacob's Pillar, which Jehovah hath blessed and hath followed Israel during all of their wan-

(101)

derings. When Joshua, the son of Nun, made a covenant with all of the tribes of Judah, this stone was
made a witness. And Joshua said unto all the people:
'Behold, this stone shall be a witness unto us, for it
hath heard all of the words of the Lord which He
spake unto us and shall, therefore, be a witness unto
you, lest ye deny your God.' This stone was brought
here by Benjamin, and by some of the workmen was
thrown into the rubbish. Have ye not read in the
Scriptures that the stone which the builders rejected
the same became the head of the corner?"

The stone was discovered by the iron ring and the
kingdom that possesses it will be an iron kingdom.

"Sovereign master, the stone lies on the northeast
corner of the arch. It is slivered by the fire, and a
crack runs through the whole length of it. I am at a
loss to know how we can raise it without injury."

"Let the cord be wound around seven times. Are
you ready?"

"I am."

"Then let us raise it, in the name of Jehovah."

By careful management on the part of the Fellow
Crafts it was raised and landed safely. It was 22 inches
long, 13 inches broad and 11 inches deep. In color it
was of a bluish gray, mixed with veins of red. The iron
rings at each end were old and rusty, while the pillow,
or pillar as it was more frequently called, showed
plainly that it had been purified, as by fire.

View of the River Nile.

"Let us now proceed to rescue the 'ark of the covenant,'" said the prophet, and immediately the Fellow Craft descended, by means of the strong cord, to the entrance of the door of the vault, for here it was secreted by the Craft the moment the walls of the city had fallen. "Sovereign Master, the cord has been wrapped around seven times in commemoration of the Sabbath of the Lord our God."

As the ark was being raised Jeremiah exclaimed: "Thus ye shall answer them, that the waters of Jordan were cut off before the ark of the covenant of the Lord when it passed over Jordan.

"And they said: 'If ye send away the ark of the God of Israel, send it not empty.'

"'And it shall come to pass, when ye be multiplied and increased in the land in those days,' saith the Lord, 'they shall say, no more the ark of the covenant of the Lord, neither shall it come to mind, neither shall they remember it, neither shall they visit it, neither shall that be done any more.'

"This is the ark, my brethren, wherein is deposited the stone tablets that Moses wrote upon the mount. It was made to receive them and nothing else, and in the later ages, when our brotherhood shall bring it forth from its secret hiding-place on Israelitish soil, the whole land will be filled with the glory of our God. Then shall Judah go before Israel into Jerusalem. Then shall they look upon Him whom they have pierced and

mourn for Him as an only son.   Then, my brethren, if
they hear not Moses and the prophets, neither would
they be persuaded though one rose from the dead."

At this moment there appeared in the midst of them
a man in shining raiment, clothed as with the sun, and
said : " Peace be unto you."   Fear came upon them.
Was not this he who appeared unto Jacob when the
pillar was consecrated to the Lord?   Was not this he
who stood by Moses in the burning bush? and the
bush was nor consumed; was not this he who had
walked with the three Hebrew children through the
furnace of fire and who appeared unto Nebuchadnezzar
like unto the son of God?   Were they not standing on
holy ground?   Did not the angel of the Lord stand
here on this spot, by the side of the ark of the covenant, and stay the plague?   Then they fell prostrate
on their faces before him ; and again he said :   " Peace
be unto you."   When they looked up they were alone.
The stone! the ark!   But they too had vanished.

About a mile outside of the city walls of Jerusalem,
on the side of the Mount of Olives, there was a cave
which centuries before had been dug out and fitted in
with solid masonry, and was known as "the King's
Tomb."   It was known, however, to but few that within
the tomb was a secret passage that led to a chamber of
extraordinary beauty and design.   This chamber had
been fitted up by the Knights of the East to resemble
the lodge-room in King Solomon's Temple.   The secret

spring that threw open the massive granite rock was
known only to Jeremiah and Baruch, who were the
Grand Chaplain and the Scribe of the Order of Knights.
In years gone by it had been a lair for wild beasts, and
after that it had been occupied by a witch, whose wild
incantations had put the people to flight, and but few
dared to pass that way in the night. Hence it came to
pass that at the fall of the temple the chamber was
already a lodge-room, dedicated to the Knights of the
East. Toward this cave Jeremiah and Baruch bent
their footsteps. They were overpowered by the appearance of the angel of the Lord, and were in sore distress
at the mysterious disappearance of the ark and the
pillar.

"This is the Lord's doings, and marvelous in our
eyes," said the Seer after a long silence.

"We can only state the case to the craft as it is,"
said Baruch, "and we ought to be thankful that our
seven brethren were present, else we might be accused
by the craft of dishonesty of purpose."

"Jehovah always has eye witnesses," said the prophet.
"He never leaves His children to the mercy of man,
only for a season; but look! is not that a stranger
standing in the entrance of the cave?"

The king's path was a winding one, shaded by olive
trees, so that it was impossible for them to see even the
face of the rock, until turning a sharp angle in the path
they came directly upon him. The sun had not yet

risen, and they were at a loss to know who he could
be and the nature of his business. It was well known
by the inhabitants of Jerusalem that since the liberation
of Jeremiah and Baruch they had been living in the
King's Tomb, and it was also reported that there was a
secret understanding between Nebuchadnezzar and the
Seer, for at his command Baruch had been liberated,
and not only that, the Czar had commanded that they
be maintained from the store-house of the city. When
they returned from Egypt and took up their abode in
the cave the Jews rejoiced greatly, as they both feared
and hated the Seer. As they advanced toward the
stranger, and were about to exchange friendly salutations, his raiment was changed to lightning and his
face like unto the sun. As he stood before them they
recognized the same angel that had appeared to them
at the corner of the temple. Rooted to the spot, they
dare not look up. "Peace be unto you, for, as Noah
went forth from Ararat to found the kingdoms of the
earth, so shall you go forth from Jerusalem to found
the Kingdom of our God. Fear not. I go before you
into Joppa." When they looked up he had vanished
out of their sight.

"Why stand ye gazing up into heaven?" The
speaker had just ridden up to the mouth of the cave,
and throwing his bridle over the bough of an olive tree
sprang from his horse and confronted the two men
before they had recovered their presence of mind

sufficiently to comprehend that they were still in the land of the living and that grand work must be accomplished before they would be called hence. As soon as they recognized the young prince they were anxious to know the whereabouts of Myra and Tea Tephi, and if any mishap had befallen them. Having been assured that they were in Jerusalem, in the house of one Cornelius, a friend of the prophet, they entered the cave and sat down. Strange things had taken place during the past few months. The governor and his staff of officers had been killed by Ishmael, the princess stolen and rescued by the Ethiopian and the prince, their flight into Egypt and their hasty return to the land of their birth, but strangest of all was the mysterious disappearance of the ark and the pillar. Having related to the prince the whole of their adventures during the night, and finding he had no solution to give, the prophet touched the secret spring of the inner *sanctum sanctorum* when a flood of light burst upon him.

He arose hastily and entering the passage the door was shut by an unseen hand, and he was alone. As he passed on down the corridor the light grew brighter and brighter, there was a sound as of the rushing of many mighty waters, while heavenly music charmed his now bewildered senses. The lamb that he had placed on the altar for a sacrifice was now being consumed by a fire that was coming down from heaven, and while he looked, behold! a lion stood upon one side of the

throne and a unicorn on the other, while an eagle with
outstretched wings was standing on the top of the
throne. Advancing, he sat down, and the word of the
Lord came unto him. He saw in the vision the ark
and the pillar directly under him, and then he heard a
voice saying: "Let this seat be forever vacant from
this hour." The fire went out, the roaring ceased, the
music died away and the prophet slept as sweetly as a
child in its mother's arms. No fears for time, no fears
for eternity.

Silently Baruch and the prince came down the corridor and entered the chamber. They saw the chair occupied by God's anointed. Little did they dream that
it was given them to behold the chair occupied for the
last time. As soon as the prophet awoke it would be
vacant forever.

> " 'Tis the hour of Judah's travail,
>   'Tis the darkness of her night,
> 'Tis the time of Levi's trouble,
>   But beyond it beams the light.
> Look! the great and grand Creator
>   Hides away their ark from sight.
> Judah, Levi, thou art wanting,
>   Israel's nine proclaim the right."

CHAPTER IX.

THE ANCIENT NINE.

IN the secret chamber leading from the king's cave, wherein the "ark of the covenant" was discovered by Jeremiah, were convened nine men, whose names will be found in the ark, in the fullness of time, written in letters of blood. Happy are they who bring it forth in the name of Jehovah on that day.

The nine were now being consecrated by the prophet Jeremiah. The chamber was hung in tapestry of red, white, and blue velvet, emblazoned with nine stars. The throne in the East whereon sat the Seer was elevated by nine steps, supported by seven lions, one eagle, and centrally by a cherubim, clothed with the sun, standing upon the moon and crowned with a diadem of nine stars. In the north were five thrones, and in the south were five thrones. On the ten thrones sat nine men, one throne being vacant during all time, for on that throne sat Jeremiah when the angel of the Lord revealed to him the secret hiding-place of the ark, and who had promised to go before him on to Israelitish soil, and there show him the holy ground that would hide away from Judah that pledge that had been given them by Jehovah until the final consummation of all things. And from that hour they should say no more "the ark of the covenant."

It was to pass out of their hands and minds into the hands and minds of a lost and nameless race, who would acknowledge and bow down before "the Lord our Righteousness." For, says Jeremiah, "In his days Judah shall be saved and Israel shall dwell safely, and this is his name whereby he shall be called." On the throne in the East sat Jeremiah. Over his head was a chain of gold having three links. In the left-hand link was the name Judah written in Hebrew; in the right, Israel, written in Greek; and in the central link was a lamb, with his head reclining on Jacob's pillar. Over these links were three mottoes. Over the one on the left was written: "We have slain the Lamb." Over the Lamb was written: "Before Abraham was I am." At the right, over the head of Israel, was written: "For the Lord hath chosen Jacob unto Himself, and Israel for His peculiar treasure." Seated in the south were Baruch and Eochaid the prince, while the seven were Israelites of the house of Benjamin. The order would from that hour be known as "The Ancient Nine."

When Jeremiah arose the eyes of the nine were riveted upon the man whom angels delighted to honor. From underneath the folds of his white robe he drew forth a silver lancet; then, baring his arm, he pierced a vein, and taking up a tiny golden inkstand he allowed the blood to trickle drop by drop into it until it was full then severing the vein, he bound up the wound with a silken scarf. And now, as he turns his eyes toward heaven, he seemed about to be translated, and thus he spoke : " The oracles that were born in Eden have been faithfully transmitted down through the generations from father to son through secret signs, grips, and passwords, up to the building of the pyramid, under the guiding hand of our grand master Job ; thence onward to the building of the temple under the ruling power of our two worthy and most exalted masters Hiram king of Tyre, and Hiram Abif, thence onward to this hour. The seven are called together to add to their number two more, making you, at the close of this conclave, ' The Ancient Nine,' to keep in remembrance the secret hiding-place of the ' Ark of our God.' Happy are the nine who, in the latter days, shall bear the ark back again to our fallen city and countrymen. And you hereby most solemnly swear, that you will keep and conceal the secret place of the ark of the Most High God, revealing it to none save him that hath been appointed to fill the place of a dead brother. And you hereby solemnly swear that none of the tribe of Judah, or of the tribe of Levi, shall ever be a member of your conclave. The ark to them is lost. In future generations, wherever they may wander, there will be no remembrance of the ark. Their synagogues will be void of it ; they will remember it no more, for this is the

sacred link that binds Israel to the Branch, 'The Lord
our Righteousness.' All nations of the earth in process
of time will sit in secret conclave one after another, as
ages succeed ages, save Judah and Levi; they, and
they only, are forever debarred from an entrance into
your council. The vacant chair will remind you that
all prophecy must be fulfilled. That seat must be forever vacant. It will remind you, also, that from underneath that chair went forth the ark to be buried on
Israelitish soil. It will remind you that Jeremiah of
the fated tribes was its last occupant. Let the ark be
brought forth."

Silently as the angel of death guards the departing
spirit of the cherubim, so in like manner was the ark
lifted from its hiding-place and set upon the golden
table, in the chancel before the throne. All heads were
bowed, for before them lay the corpse of Judah. Their
last king was no more. Their throne and their ark was
to be transplanted till the end of time. Judah's God
was from that moment Israel's God. The Branch, the
Mediator, "was not sent only to the lost sheep of the
house of Israel." Silently each man signed his name
in the blood of the prophet, silently it was placed
within the ark, and silently the lid of the casket closed
until the fulfillment of all the laws and the prophets.
Then the voice of the Seer rang out through the arches
of the chamber: "The first great duty of Masons
when convened?"

" To see that we are duly guarded."

" Attend to that duty, and inform the guard that I am about to close this conclave in the name of Jehovah. And now may the God of our fathers, Abraham, Isaac, and Jacob, with the Lord our Righteousness as Mediator, be with you, both now and forever. So mote it be."

After leaving the conclave, the young prince wandered down the mountain pass lost in profound meditation. His thoughts went over the past history of the Jewish nation. Momentous scenes had been enacted in Babylon during the past few years. He saw in his mind the three Hebrew worthies cast into a fiery furnace, and lo, the fourth appeared, like unto the Son of God. They had walked forth without the smell of fire on their garments. They had refused to bow down to the golden god set up by Nebuchadnezzar, and their God had delivered them.

Who were the prophets, and whence came their power? Jeremiah had prophesied the downfall of the Jewish kingdom and the destruction of Jerusalem, and lo! these things came to pass. He saw Daniel a captive, slave, through the interpretation of a dream, made ruler over the whole province of Babylon. And then this same Daniel had prophesied that the Czar should be driven forth, and for the space of seven years eat grass like the oxen, before he would acknowledge the true God of the Hebrews, and, verily, in that same

year the prophecy was fulfilled. Then his thoughts
flew back over the history of this peculiar people. He
saw the waters of the River Jordan divide ; he saw
Joshua, with his sword raised on high, command the sun
and moon to stand still ; he saw Samson draw a living
fountain of water from the jaw-bone of an ass ; he saw
Moses, at the head of three millions of people, standing
on the shore of the Red Sea ; he saw at his command
the waters flow back from their places and dry land
appear ; he saw that mighty host pass over dry-shod.
" Lift thou up thy rod and stretch out thine hand over
the sea and divide it, and the children of Israel shall go
on dry land through the midst of the sea." Did the
waters congeal ? No. For was not this a semi-tropical
climate ? Again, he saw Pharaoh and his hosts in hot
pursuit ; he saw them enter the same road to cross the
sea ; he saw on the other shore Moses raise his staff
on high, and Pharaoh and his hosts were drowned in
the sea. He heard the glad cry echo and re-echo, bound
and rebound from shore to shore, " The horse and the
rider hath he thrown into the sea." He saw the ten
plagues, visited one after another through the command
of Moses, smiting the Egyptians and bringing upon them
ruin and death. And then his thoughts flew back to
Joseph, once a captive slave like Daniel, and like him
through the interpretation of a dream made ruler over
Egypt. From whence came they ? Were they not orig-
inally of the same kindred, blood, and tongue as the

Chaldeans? Yes, for he saw Abraham coming up out of
Chaldea, to become the father of this peculiar people.
Who then was the God of the Hebrews? Was he not
a God of the Chaldean and the Egyptian? Was he
not a God of the Ethiopian from Nubia, even unto
Abyssinia. Again, he saw them forced to endure all
the toils and privations of a common slave. He saw
them purloining all the golden jewelry prior to their
exodus; he saw them wandering for forty years; he
saw the whole three millions cut down out of time,
save Caleb and Joshua; he saw Jerusalem overthrown,
the temple pillaged, the Hebrews again in bondage,
while the holy vessels that the Czar had taken from
the temple were at that moment being debased by unholy hands. Again, he saw Zedekiah, bound hand and
foot in fetters of brass, standing before the king, who
at his command was made sightless forever. He saw
his family cut down before him; he saw Judah debased.
But the seed of Judah could never die. God's covenant with David was as enduring as the everlasting
hills. " Hark!"

A crackling of the brush attracted his attention, but
before he could draw his sword from the scabbard he
was borne down to the earth, a mantle was thrown over
his head, and he was bound hand and foot. Then one
of the ruffians stooped down and, bending over him,
hissed in his ear, "Give me the secret word of the
Mystic Brotherhood and your life will be spared. Re-

fuse, and by the powers of darkness you shall die the death."

The prince knew too well that his hour had come. His thoughts went out to the beautiful princess Tea Tephi, whom he had rescued from the hands of her enemies. Why had he not spoken to her of his great love, that she might weep over his coffin. Now he must die uncared for on a foreign shore. Rather ten thousand deaths than the betrayal of his masonic vows. "I have but one answer," said the prince, as soon as the mantle was withdrawn so that he could breathe. "And that," hissed the assassin?

"Never!"

"Then die!"

"Hist! some one approaches. Let us bear the body to the lower dungeon, peradventure the lamp has not yet gone out."

CHAPTER X.

THE DUNGEON.

WHEN the prince returned to consciousness he found himself in a dark loathsome dungeon, lying on the cold, slimy floor, without even a straw for a pillow to rest his aching head and throbbing temples. He tried to rise, but he found he could not. There were strange and grating noises in his head; his brain was on fire; he was dying of thirst. Oh for just one drop of water; then he could die in peace. But alas, there was no hope. The fever burned, and now he began to talk wildly and to beat his head against the walls of his prison, crying loudly for the princess he loved so well. But the walls yielded back to him only the echo of his own voice. How long he had been in the dungeon he knew not. He only knew that darkness, like the Egyptian darkness, which could be felt, was hovering over his brain, and that in a few short hours he would stand in the presence of Jeremiah's God. He had never prayed, but now he felt his soul lifted up to a great white throne, where innumerable angels ministered unto those who had been faithful to their trust. Had he not been faithful even in the hands of the assassin? Was he not at that moment asking himself the question, if God was

not a God of all.   Oh if he could but see once more his
friend the prophet, he would lead him, even as a little
child is led by his father, into the true path of eternal
life.   He must not die.   He would not die.

Again he tried to raise himself, while the fever
burned into a flame that would consume him, even as
the fire that came down from heaven consumed the
sacrifice.   How long he lay thus he knew not, but it
seemed to him like an eternity of years.

At last the door of the dungeon is thrown open by
the Ethiopian, and by the flickering rays of the lantern
he sees a prisoner lying on the floor in a death-like
stupor.   As he comes nearer, and the rays of the light
fall on the face of the prisoner, he starts back in affright.
Merciful God, it is Eochaid the prince.   Tenderly he
raises him up in his arms, and bears him down through
the passage to an open court, then on through another
passage and through another court until he comes to
the house of Cornelius.   Here he calls loudly for help.
The door is quickly thrown open, and the stalwart Ethiopian bears his burden up the winding stairs to an airy
chamber, that is being hastily prepared for his reception; then, laying him down, he presses a sponge filled
with water to his lips, he bathes his head with water,
he applies the blisters, and still the patient remains in
a death-like trance, while the fever burns.

Seeing that nothing more could be done, he called
the princess, and hastened away toward the cave.

DR. TALMAGE BAPTIZING IN THE RIVER JORDAN.

Méeting the Seer and Baruch coming down the mount, he tells them of the finding of the prince and of the death-struggle now going on in the house of Cornelius, and bids them hasten, or it will be too late.

Within the sick chamber Myra and Tea Tephi were doing all in their power to alleviate the suffering of the prince. Now he rouses up and calls loudly to be released from the dungeon, then he calls for water. Again he calls loudly for Jeremiah, to show him the true path that will lead him to the God of the Hebrews. Then his voice dies away, and they hear him murmur the name of Tea Tephi. Now she knows that he loves her. He had never plighted his vows, but now her heart goes out to him as it had never gone out to another. She knows now that she would go with him to the ends of the earth, and if, as Jeremiah had spoken, she, and she only, was to continue the house of Judah, who was there in all of the wide, wide world that could fill his place. "O Jeremiah, Jeremiah, hasten and save him. Thou hast the faith that will open the very gates of heaven. Angels delight to honor thee. Thy power at the foot of the throne will save him."

But still the fever rages and the spark of life flickers in its casket. Will it go out? "Hark!" Jeremiah is in prayer. The windows of heaven are opened, the great white throne appears, angels and archangels stoop down to listen, while the flood-gates of God's love have covered the house like a mantle. The throne! The

Lamb! Speak, O God, and he shall be healed. And now a great calm comes over the prince, and he sleeps. The voice of the prophet dies away, the twilight comes on, the night grows into morning, the sun rises over the craggy peaks of the Mount of Olives, and still she watches and the prince sleeps. Will he awake clothed and in his right mind? Hope on, sweet maiden, for the prophet sleeps.

Were he not assured that his prayer had been answered, he would be standing at the bedside of the dying prince, comforting you in your sorrow. But he knows now that two hearts have been made as one. He has seen in the distance the fruition of all his hopes. He knows that Eochaid has accepted David's God, and that in him the kingdom of Israel has a firm foundation.

"Tea Tephi." The prince has awakened, and as he calls her name he stretches forth his hand, and she places her own in his.

"Where am I?"

"You are in the house of Cornelius, you have been very sick with a fever, but you are better now; do not try to talk, but sleep and rest."

"Oh I have had such a beautiful dream. I thought I was in my father's palace, and you were with me, and together we built a beautiful temple. When it was finished, Jeremiah and Baruch dedicated it to your God. Then Jeremiah blessed us, and we became his children. Then we ruled the kingdom, and it became great and powerful, and all nations looked to us for help, because we had the ark of the covenant secreted on our soil and Jacob's pillar in our temple. Then there appeared an angel unto me, and said if we were Judah we must be crowned upon it or we could not reign over Israel. Then we were crowned, and the men and women carried palms in their hands, and the children carried flowers, which they strewed in our pathway, while all of the people waved their palms and shouted 'Long live the house of Zedekiah, the seed royal of the house of David.' Will you go with me to my island home to share with me my joys and my sorrows? Speak now, that I may sleep to awake to a new life."

The answer was given, the pledges sealed, and the prince slept.

After Eochaid had been struck down by the ruffians, he was taken in the arms of two of the gang and borne rapidly away toward the city. Meeting the Ethiopian on his way to the prophet's cave, they told him they had found a man who had fallen by the wayside, and they were bearing him into the city. When the Ethiopian arrived at the cave, where he should have met the prince, his suspicions were aroused, and he blamed himself for not having taken a look at the sick man he had met, so he hastened back to Jerusalem, to find out if possible where the prince lodged. He knew almost every one in the city, as he had been a favorite slave of king Zedekiah, and now he was a

favorite with them all, since Zedekiah was a captive. He
knew every dungeon and vault underneath the palace,
but he had no suspicion that there could be any prison-
ers in the dungeon, as he had, by the command of Nebuchadnezzar, thrown open all of the doors. He, however, thought it would do no harm to make an investigation, as something he had heard drop from one of
the hostlers made him fear that the prince had been
waylaid by the gang, who were determined to wrench
the password from a master mason, and he knew that
Eochaid was a mason of high rank; and if he had been
murdered by the men around the palace no better place
than one of the dungeons could be found for the con-
cealment of the victim, hence his search and his horror
in finding the prince.

He now determined to bring the guilty men to judg-
ment, and accordingly informed the hostler that he had
found the prince, and that he was then in a condition
to reveal to them the password of a mason. The four
men, thinking that the slave was anxious to gain possession of the password, followed him down through
the lower passages to the dungeon wherein they had
cast the prince. The Ethiopian unlocked the door and
told them to enter. As soon as the last one passed into
the cell, the door was shut upon them, the key turned
in the lock, the bolts shot back into their sockets, and
they were left to suffer the extreme penalty of an
Ethiopian law.

CHAPTER XI.

DEATH OF MYRA.

THE creaking of the windlass, the clanking of chains, the flapping of the sails, all told the travelers that they were starting on a long journey to the home of the "Occidental Prince." Seated in the cabin of the ship was Jeremiah and Baruch. The prince, with Myra and Tea Tephi, were watching the sailors on deck hoist the sails, and were listening to that peculiar cry of the sailor as the anchor came up out of the muddy water and was secured to the side of the ship.

The Ethiopian was helping the sailors, as they all admired him on account of his prowess in the recent combat against the men of Ishmael.

"You had better look the chart over carefully," said the Seer, "so that there can be no mistake. You must remember that we are leaving the seven here in Jerusalem, and death might sweep us three away before we could accomplish our purpose. I am satisfied that the ark and pillar will arrive safely, for God has so ordered, and His promises are as enduring as the everlasting hills. Man faileth and returneth back to dust, but the word of God is both sure and steadfast."

"The chart seems to be imperfect," said Baruch.

"Ah, and that very imperfection is what covers our

secret. Man's salvation will be brought about through his imperfection. ' Behold the man is become as one of us, to know good and evil,' transformed him from the son of man to the son of God. From earthly to heavenly; for, says Eve on the birth of Cain, ' I have gotten a man from the Lord,' and again on the birth of Seth, from which sprang our race, ' For God hath appointed me another seed instead of Abel, whom Cain slew.' Cain and his posterity were destroyed; Seth saved through Noah. From our imperfections sprang the promise of a Redeemer. I had rather be a sinner with that knowledge than be perfect without it, for angels fall, and hence immortal man fell; but the very moment they partook of the fruit of the tree of knowledge, that moment they became heirs of heaven through the promised blood of a Saviour, and through that blood must remain redeemed forever."

At this moment the prince came into the saloon, and hearing the prophet speaking upon the subject of the fall of man, desired to know more.

"After God created Adam and Eve," said the Seer, "He blessed them, and said unto them, ' Be fruitful and multiply, and replenish the earth, and subdue it.' And God saw everything that He had made, and behold! it was very good. From that day until they partook of the fruit of the tree of knowledge was no doubt thousands of years, for the earth was densely inhabited."

" How do you know that ? "

"From the facts. First, 'And Adam called his wife's name Eve, because she was the mother of all the living.' This was before God made coats of skin to clothe them. And, second, Cain said, 'I shall be a fugitive and a vagabond in the earth, and it shall come to pass that every one that findeth me shall slay me.' This proves that there were thousands of people in the earth at that time. These were a race of immortals, so far as death was concerned, for death had not been passed upon man, in that man had not sinned, and it was a matter of impossibility for man to sin without a knowledge of good and evil. Thus, on the day that Adam partook of the fruit of the tree, on that day he became a dying mortal, and from that day he lived nine hundred and thirty years, and he died. Prior to that time he had no age, in that he had not sinned. The next birth after the so-called fall of man was Cain, who was born under the ban of death, and hence he is called a man from the Lord. Here we have two distinct races of men. Now when the sons of God saw the daughters of men, that they were fair, they began to inter-marry, which produced the third race. Now we have three distinct classes of people, viz.: those under the law, those without the law, and those born in a positive and negative condition. It was this act that determined the Lord to destroy the earth and bring us through the loins of Seth."

"Why do you think they were immortal?"

"Because God said: 'My spirit shall not always strive with man, for that he also is flesh,' meaning that while he was not under the law of death he was flesh and blood, like those born in sin, and hence He would give them one hundred and twenty years. At that time the ark would be completed and He would destroy them with a flood. Job says: 'Hast thou marked the old way which wicked men have trodden, which were cut down out of time, whose foundations were overflown with a flood, which said unto God, "Depart from us," and "What can the Almighty do for them?"'"

"If, as you say, they were immortal, how then were they destroyed?"

"They were not, only in a bodily form; they inhabit the world to-day, entering into men and women. They tried to enter the body of Moses, but durst not bring a railing accusation against him. Since the destruction of the earth by the flood they are afraid of the water, and hence walk in dry places. In Jerusalem the people test even the dogs. If a dog is afraid of the water he is immediately killed, as his fear of the water leads the people to suppose he has a mad spirit."

"Why do they think it is one of those spirits that has entered the dog?"

"Because if the dog bites you, then you in turn go mad at the sight of water."

"What will be their final end?"

"Their doom is no resurrection. Isaiah says of them:

'O Lord, our God, other lords beside Thee have had dominion over us, but by Thee only will we make mention of Thy name; they are dead; they shall not live; they are deceased; they shall not rise. Therefore Thou hast visited and destroyed them, and made all of their memory to perish.' Again the Psalmist says: 'I have said ye are gods, and all of you are the children of the Most High, but ye shall die like men.' Thus you will notice that when God gave the commandments to Moses, the first was: 'Thou shalt have no other gods before Me.'"

"If, as you say, death had not been passed upon men, in that men had not sinned, how then were they accountable?"

"That was brought to pass through inter-marriage. They produced a race that were mortal and immortal; with the law and without the law; with the promise of a Redeemer and without the promise; and hence Job says: 'Now what can the Almighty do for them?' Those of Adam's race that were born without sin perished without sin, and hence no condemnation. But the giants who were born from the sons of God and the daughters of men were left without a Redeemer, and hence no resurrection. When Shiloh comes he will go into the prisons and preach to the spirits, and from that point they will cease to become the torments of men. Then the kingdom of our Lord will be founded. 'Peace on earth, good will towards men.'"

"And are two kingdoms to be set up?" asked the prince.

"Yes; one temporal and the other spiritual. Shiloh will come to Jerusalem to suffer and die at the hands of his brethren. He will rise again, thereby making the resurrection of the dead an immortal truth. He will then go to the lost sheep of the house of Israel, and they will accept the pledge, and through them in process of time the whole world will be brought to a knowledge of the glory of our God. This is the true secret of Abraham's call up out of Chaldea. The sons of Noah trampled all laws under their feet, and hence God made for Himself, through the seed of Abraham, Israel His peculiar treasure."

"And how will the world know it is Israel if they lose their name and identity?"

"Ah, therein is the blessing concealed. The righteous man giveth without letting the right hand know what the left hand doeth. If state and war secrets were known the kingdom would be overthrown. God's movements are mysterious; the young and noble are taken, while the aged and decrepid are left in their sorrow. Judah will be known throughout all time, and from that simple fact they will be bereft of power. Their only safety in ages to come will be within the gates of their brethren."

"And will they know them?"

"No, not fully, until the ark is brought forth by our

brotherhood, and they look upon Him whom they have pierced."

At this moment the door was thrown open, and Myra, leaning on the arm of the Ethiopian, came into the saloon. A palor overspread her countenance which the Ethiopian said was caused by the action of the waves, but the prophet shook his head. For the first time it came over him like a flash of lightning that never had he seen her in his visions of the foreign shore. It was Tea Tephi, and she was always alone. In his visions of Jerusalem the two maidens were always together. Was she about to join her father's family?

During the day the ship doctor came, and after a careful examination passed out of the stateroom with a troubled look that did not escape the notice of either the prophet or the prince. Tea Tephi had not been informed of the condition of the princess, she supposing it was from the effects of the choppy sea, that is confined almost entirely to lakes and seas, but the time had now come when the maiden must be informed of the dangerous condition of Myra. Accordingly the prophet bade the Ethiopian summon her to the deck.

When the princess came up she scanned the features of the prophet for some sign whereby she might divine the nature of his call, but she could not read his face. As she sat down beside him he took her hand in his own and said:

"My daughter, in the city of the New Jerusalem there are no sieges; neither is there sword, nor famine, nor pestilence. The people there learn war no more. Your brothers and sisters all fell by the sword, save two. Ishmael will meet the Chaldean hosts, in the country of Ammon, and will perish in like manner, as others perished at his hand. Myra must soon join them, and you and you only will stand alone, the representative of Judah's God. His throne must be established. The seed of David will rule forever; God hath declared it. Let us go down now, as the hour is at hand."

When the prophet entered the sick-room his countenance was lit up with a halo of glory. Taking the hand of Myra in his own, he looked up to heaven and commanded the blessing of Judah's God to rest upon her. A sweet and heavenly calm came over the countenance of the princess, while she repeated from the Psalms of David:

"Yea, though I walk through the valley of the shadow of death, I will fear no evil, for Thou art with me; Thy rod and Thy staff they comfort me."

"Look! The gates of the city of the New Jerusalem are open. Behold my mother standing upon the battlements of heaven, with outstretched arms, awaiting to welcome me home, to go no more out forever. The angel of death hovers over me; I see the shadow of his wings, but beyond the shadow is everlasting day.

I come! I come! Hark! David calls me home. He
knows that my beautiful sister will become the mother
of nations, while I will become as his little child, wandering through the green pastures and beside the still
waters of which he spoke, guarded by cherubims and
seraphims, listening to the heavenly music of angels
and archangels, guided by the hand of my mother up
to the throne of David's God. I come! I come!"

Silently the angel hovers nearer and nearer. Slowly
the shadow of death falls like a mantle over her brow,
gradually it sinks lower and lower, until it kisses the
lips of the dying princess, while her spirit wings its
flight into realms of everlasting day. The sunbeams
faded away into twilight, night stole into morning,
when a broken-hearted company stood by the side of
the rail of the ship, preparatory to consigning all that
was mortal of Myra into the bosom of the great deep.
A stillness like that unto death came over them as they
stood beside the sleeper. Jeremiah held a book in his
hand, and from the pages he read:

"Surely He hath borne our griefs and carried our
sorrows. He is despised and rejected of men. He was
wounded for our transgressions. He was bruised for
our iniquities, and with His stripes we are healed. All
we, like sheep, have gone astray. He is brought as a
lamb to the slaughter, and as a sheep before her
shearers is dumb, so he opened not his mouth."

Gently the body was raised over the side of the ship.

A movement of the waters and Myra was at rest. And from her grave went forth little curling waves that rippled around the ship, thence onward and backward until they kissed the shores of both thrones, a link in the chain that would never be severed until the thrones were again united in the city of Jerusalem.

CHAPTER XII.

TARA.

" THE flags seem to be half-mast," said the Ethiopian, as they neared the bay of Drogheda on the northeast coast of Ireland. The people have sighted the ship, and are swarming upon the house-tops and on the quays. The prince's flag was flying at the masthead, so that all the people knew that the prince was near his native shore. As the ship entered the harbor and came up to her anchorage the flags were all run up to the peak ; then there went up a shout that was echoed and re-echoed through the length and breadth of the island. " The king is dead, long live the king."

For the moment the prince seemed to be overpowered by the news of his father's death. He had left him in perfect health, only to return and find him numbered among the dead. Thousands had now gathered upon the banks of the river, until they seemed to be like the sands of the seashore for multitude.

Never had the prophet witnessed such a sight, even in his Oriental home. Here all was love and devotion ; there all riot and confusion. Here the city was decked with flags of rejoicing ; there it was draped in the emblems of mourning. Here the people were

waiting to receive their king with outstretched arms
and an overflowing heart ; there, bereft of home, family,
and friends, bowed down with sorrow and with chains,
awaiting in darkness and despair the dread summons
that will call him to his silent home. Why this difference? And yet "hath not the potter power over
the clay, of the same lump, to make one vessel unto
honor and another unto dishonor?" Oh, joy, thou
art indeed the twin sister of sorrow! Wealth and
poverty, sickness and health, good and evil, light and
darkness, life and death, all seem bound together by a
strange fatality. As the barge moved up the river the
multitude that thronged the shores on either side rent
the air with one prolonged shout, that settled into a
roar like that of a coming tempest. Hundreds of thousands had gathered in and around the city and temple
to welcome and crown their king. When the barge
landed and the procession moved up towards the hall,
the prince and princess were preceded by Jeremiah
and Baruch, while before them were four powerful
" Knights of the East " bearing the sacred stone, upon
which rested the ark of the covenant covered with a
mantle of royal purple. Before them were children
strewing flowers over their pathway, while all the people waved their palms and shouted, " Long live the
king !"

Thus the procession moved on up to the throne.
And now a death-like stillness came over that mighty

host. Jeremiah had joined the hands of the prince and princess over the sacred stone and the ark of the covenant, and looking up toward Heaven, he commanded the blessing of Israel's God to rest upon the throne of David. " For thus saith the Lord : I will overturn, overturn, overturn it, and it shall be no more until he comes whose right it is, and I will give it to him."

" How long, O Lord, how long ! " will be the cry of Judah wandering up and down the earth without a home, while nations are vieing one with another as to which can be the most cruel and unjust toward them, restraining their liberty, confiscating their property, and banishing them from one country to another. " A race without a leader, a people without a king, a country without a government, a synagogue without a Redeemer. Famine, earthquake, sword, pestilence, death. But the seed of Judah shall reign over the house of Israel forever. God hath spoken, for from the loins of Judah shall come 'the prince of the house of David,' who will save his people. The people that should be the most exalted, crushed under the feet of nations and kingdoms, until Israel opens wide her gates and bids them enter. Here, free from persecution, they will await the morning of their redemption." " Give us wisdom to fulfill the last of all the laws and the prophets—that of hiding away from sight the broken column of Judah and the chain that binds Israel to the

Branch." " Hasten the time when Ephraim and Manasseh shall discover the people that wrought miracles
through the power of God, living miracles for the truth
of all the laws and the prophets."

The prayer ceased, and now there went up a mighty
shout, " The King and Queen are crowned!" and as
the roar died away the last words of the prophet were
taken up by the multitude, and echoed from the " centre all round to the sea." " What God hath joined
together, let no man put asunder."

Tara at this time was full of ancient castles, which had
weathered the storms and sleets of the country for hundreds of years, but the pride of the Celtic chieftain was
Tara's Hall. " Here the harp had rung out its blessing
since the days of David, for it was at that time that the
first harp was transported to Ireland by the tribe of
Dan." " Ancient Tara was situated in the county of
Meath, which at that time was in the province of Ulster, on the northeast coast of Ireland. Tara's Hall
was on the banks of the River Boyne, between Drogheda and Slane." It was nine hundred feet square,
and admittance was through twelve wings, twelve
porches, and twelve doors, a fitting emblem of the
sacred sound of three times three. The banquet-hall
contained seats for twelve hundred guests. Here the
musicians played the harp that would make the hall
famous when, like their temple at Jerusalem, it had become a heap.

When the ceremonies were all ended and the sound of revelry began, the prince together with the prophet and Baruch quietly left the hall, and entering a narrow passageway the prince touched a secret spring ; the massive granite rock swung round on its pivot, the three men entered, and the door was shut. The second empire was founded.

"And He shall set up an ensign for the nations, and shall assemble the outcasts of Israel, and gather together the dispersed of Judah from the four corners of the earth. The envy also of Ephraim shall depart and the adversaries of Judah shall be cut off. Ephraim shall not envy Judah, and Judah shall not vex Ephraim." "Behold, I lay in Zion, for a foundation, a stone, a tried stone, a precious corner-stone, a sure foundation." "Let them give glory unto the Lord and declare His praise in the islands." "And all thy children shall be taught of the Lord." "And it shall come to pass in that day that the Lord shall give thee rest from thy sorrow, and from thy fear, and from thy hard bondage, wherein thou wast made to serve. Yet the number of the children of Israel shall be as the sands of the sea-shore, that cannot be measured nor numbered ; and it shall come to pass that in the place where it was said ye are not my people, there it shall be said unto them, ye are the sons of the Living God."

It was midnight ; not a sound broke the silence save the breathing of the three men who were lowering the

ark of the covenant into its resting-place, to remain con
cealed until Judah should bow before the Lord.   When
the last rites were accomplished and the grave covered,
the prophet spoke.   " In years to come this act will be
commemorated by our brotherhood with a rap of three
times three.· Millions will sound that alarm, and yet
not know the resting-place of the ark nor yet the origin of that sound.   In due time the Lord our righteousness will appear and found His kingdom ; and so
we, in a glorious expectation of that event, bury Judah's
hope.   We, as the three selected to bury this precious
memento of the loving-kindness of our God, consign it
to the earth in the name of Jehovah, our Redeemer,
and that sacred spirit that is ever with us, planting this
sprig of shamrock over it, thereby ever holding in remembrance the sacred symbol of three times three.   In
years to come, when this kingdom shall have been overthrown and given to another: when the sacred stone
has been wrenched from them and put upon another
throne ; when their spiritual power has been transferred
to the city of the seven hills ; when that hierarchy shall
cause to flow throughout the earth oceans of blood,
then will our brotherhood hear a voice from heaven
saying, ' Let there be light,' and from that light will
spring investigation, and from investigation education,
and from education revelation, that will trample the
three great powers of darkness, viz. : ignorance, bigotry, and superstition, into the dust.   Then will that

power become antagonistic toward Masonry. But their
hour will have come, their sun will have set.   Millions
will investigate the light of Masonry, and sweep the
seven hills with the besom of destruction.   Investigation against ignorance, education against superstition,
revelation against bigotry, light against darkness. The
foundation-stone of Masonry is brotherly love, and investigation will reveal, to the astonishment of nations,
that while millions have gone down through the power
of that tyrant which professed to be founded upon
' Peace on earth, good-will toward men,' not one single
authenticated death will ever be laid at our door, and
yet we will have numbered hundreds of millions, thousands of years before this hierarchy had an existence.
Power in the hands of a temple or synagogue, controlled by superstitious bigots, is a dangerous thing ;
and hence our order to bring into the world more light,
and this will be brought to pass only when secondary
powers are subject to national laws, when liberty of
conscience and freedom of speech have secured a
firm foundation.   This can only come through education.   May the blessing of Israel's God rest upon Judah's hope until the blast of the trumpet shall call their
scattered remnant back to Jerusalem to look upon Him
whom they have pierced. ' Behold, thou art called a
Jew and resteth in the law.' Now we, brethren, as
Isaac was, are the children of promise, ' To redeem
them that were under the law, that we might receive

the adoption of sons.'   These are the two covenants,
the one from. Mount Sinai : ' For in those days the
house of Judah shall walk with the house of Israel, for
I have made a convenant with my chosen, I have sworn
unto David my servant; thy seed will I establish forever, and build up thy throne to all generations.'
Selah. ' Who are Israelites, to whom pertaineth the
adoption, and the glory, and the covenants, and the
giving of the law, and the service of God, and the
promises.' ' For they are not all Israel which are of
Israel.' Let us pray. ' Thou, O God, knowest our
down-sittings and uprisings, and understandest our
thoughts afar off.   Shield and protect us from the evil
intentions of our enemies, and support us in the troubles
and trials we are destined to endure while traveling
through this vale of tears. Man that is born of woman is
of few days and full of trouble.   He cometh forth like a
flower and is cut down ; he fleeth also as a shadow
and continueth not.   Seeing his days are determined,
the number of his months are with Thee ; Thou hast
appointed a bound that he cannot pass ; turn from him,
O God, that he may rest till he shall have accomplished
his day.   For there is hope of a tree if it be cut down
that it shall sprout again, and the tender branches
thereof shall not cease ; but man dieth and wasteth
away ; yea, man dieth and giveth up the ghost, and
where is he ?   As the waters fail from the sea and the
floods decayeth and drieth up, so man lieth down, and

riseth not again till the heavens be no more ; he shall
not awake out of his sleep. Yet, O Lord, have compassion upon the children of thy creation, and save
them with an everlasting salvation ! ' 'So mote it
be.' Let us away, the night grows into morning."

Taking a southwesterly course, a two hours' journey
brought them directly to the northeast corner of the
hall. They had described a perfect triangle, with the
ark resting at the northeast corner.

" Is this thy funeral pyre, thy lonely grave,
 Oh, ancient Tara, city once so fair ?
Where are thy halls and palaces so brave,
 Thy sons and daughters, strong and beauteous, where ?
Great wast thou in olden time—a sacred place.
 Here reigned wise kings in great Jehovah's name ;
Here shone an aged prophet's honored face ;
 Here to be taught the rude barbarians came ;
Here rests the ark of God,
 The holiest thing within thy spreading bounds ;
But thou hast perished,
 Thy sacred relics lie unsought, unfound ;
And midst the buried arches, pillars prone,
And fragments huge. of hewn and carven stone,
I search, and lo ! in a dim nook behold
The Ark of shittim wood, o'erlaid with gold,
 And shadowed by the wings of cherubims."

Author unknown.

CHAPTER XIII.

DEATH OF JEREMIAH AND BARUCH.

" As age creeps on the time flies fast,
Days, months, and years glide by,
And each seem shorter than the last,
And swifter seems to fly."

TEN years had passed, and Jeremiah was now old
and well stricken in years. The sceptre of Judah had
not departed, nor had his prophecies come to naught.
Baruch had seen in a vision his beloved son Zacharias
slain in the temple by the Idumeans, and he was now
prepared to return to Egypt. The prophecies concerning Baruch must soon be fulfilled, and Jeremiah also
must in the fulfillment of prophecy return to the birth-
place of Ephraim and Manasseh, for God had declared
that he would punish them in that place. Bethshemesh, the home of Joseph and Asenath, the university
of all arts and sciences, the birthplace of all sacred liter-
ature, the college of Moses and Aaron, the temple
erected to celebrate victory over death, the misfortunes
and triumphs of Joseph, the trials and prophecies of
Moses, and the final destruction of the enemies of Israel,
all rose up before Jeremiah, beckoning his body onward
to the tomb and his spirit upward to the throne of
God.

(146)

The young prince and princess which had been born unto Eochaid were now Jeremiah's sole companions. From him they had learned the true path of wisdom, in that they worshiped the God of the Hebrews. The parting from these cherubs was like unto death, but as Nebo was to Moses, as the Jordan was to Elijah, as the temple was to Samson, so in like manner Bethshemesh was unto him. There he would lie down and rise not again until the morning of the resurrection. The beautiful monument would stand on the banks of the river Nile until salvation was proclaimed throughout the length and breadth of the earth. The throne of Judah was established over Israel for ever, and Israel would sing the song of Moses and the Lamb until time should be no longer.

Nebuchadnezzar had despoiled Egypt and slain Ishmael, as Jeremiah had prophesied, and was now the virtual ruler. An edict signed by him was in the possession of both Jeremiah and Baruch, bidding them go withersoever they willed.

The parting between prince and prophet was like a two-edged sword, but each knew that not one jot or tittle of the prophecies should fail. They must both return to that land where it had been said unto them, "*Enter not lest ye die.*" Now the hour had come when they must obey the edict of a higher king than Nebchadnezzar. Raising his hands, Jeremiah commanded the blessing of God to rest upon the new covenant. ·

"Behold the days come, saith the Lord, that I will make a new covenant with the house of Israel and with the house of Judah.

"Not according to the covenant made with their fathers in the day that I took them by the hand, to bring them out of the land of Egypt, which my covenant they break, although I was a husband unto them, saith the Lord.

"But this shall be the covenant that I will make with the house of Israel: After those days, saith the Lord, I will put my law in their inward parts, and write it in their hearts, and will be their God, and they shall be my people.

"And they shall teach no more every man his neighbor, and every man his brother, saying: Know the Lord, for they shall all know me, from the least of them unto the greatest of them, saith the Lord; for I will forgive their iniquity, and I will remember their sins no more.

"Thus saith the Lord, which giveth the sun for a light by day, and the ordinances of the moon and of the stars for a light by night, which divideth the sea when the waves thereof roar; the Lord of Hosts is His name.

"If those ordinances depart from before me, saith the Lord; then the seed of Israel also shall cease from being a nation before me forever."

Thus spake Jeremiah, as he and Baruch went forth

from Ireland into Egypt to meet their God. As they passed up the river Nile, the thoughts of Jeremiah wandered back to the days of Joseph when he controlled the granaries of Egypt. Now he sees in the future seed of Joseph—Manasseh—the great people controlling the granaries of the world.

He sees Moses, at the head of the children of Israel, led by the hand of God up out of Egypt, and then he sees the covenant broken in pieces. Moses is not permitted to enter into the promised land, while the children of Israel have again become captives in the land of the Assyrians.

Again he sees the second covenant entered into between the Almighty and the children of Israel, which is as enduring as the everlasting hills. Their throne established until the sea gives up its dead. Now his eyes wander over the great Necropolis, among the tombs wherein were the bodies of the Pharaohs who persecuted his people.

Again he sees Azariah and Johanan lead that mighty host of Jews into Egypt, in direct defiance to the command of God, and then he sees them fall, one after another, by the sword and by the pestilence and by the famine, until not one soul is left save Baruch and him-self. He hears the doom pronounced by God Himself: "*I will punish you in this place.*"

Then he fell on his face and wept over Judah.

In the green fields of the Delta, on the banks of the

river Nile, near ancient Memphis and Cairo, stands to-day a beautiful red granite obelisk that has withstood the storms of nearly fifty centuries. This is the Bethshemesh of sacred scriptures. Here was born Asenath, the daughter of Potipherah, the priest of On, who became the mother of Ephraim and Manasseh. Here, beneath the shadow of this beautiful rosy monument, rest the ·bodies of Jeremiah the prophet and Baruch the blessed. Here they await the grand hailing sign of the Supreme Architect of the Universe. This monument has stood from the earliest infancy of Noah's race up to the present hour, and will continue on until " They shall teach no more every man his neighbor, and every man his brother, saying: Know the Lord, for they shall all know Him, from the least of them unto the greatest of them, saith the Lord."

CHAPTER XIV.

CYRUS.

KING ASTYAGES sat on his throne in a profound and sorrowful meditation. Already a jealousy had sprung up and taken root in his heart against his only daughter, the princess Mandane, for he had dreamed that she would bear a son who would overthrow the Median kingdom, and that his dominion would extend to the uttermost parts of the earth. How was he to frustrate this grand design, which had been foretold by the prophet Isaiah more than two hundred years before, was the question that perplexed and annoyed him. He had very little faith in the powers of the Persians, as they were from the loins of Shem. Media was on a direct line from Japhet, and hence he considered her proof against Persian invasion. Why not marry her to a Persian prince, and thus prevent the possibility of greatness in the sons born unto them. Yes; he would marry her to a Persian prince, and bring to naught the prophecies of Isaiah. Accordingly Cambyses was introduced into the king's palace, and an alliance was entered into between the prince and princess. Thus he had unwittingly fulfilled the first part of the prophecy,

that of joining the two kingdoms for the utter annihil-
ation of the Median throne. When the princess gave
birth to a son, the king was thrown into the greatest
state of excitement and alarm. The child must die,
even if he had to issue an edict like that unto the king
of Egypt, and he would see to it that there was no bul-
rush business, as in the case of Moses.

In this state of mind, he sent for his trusted servant
Harpagus, and ordered him to put the child to death.
Now it so happened that the wife of Harpagus had
given birth to a son on that same day, and the heart
of the servant was touched with compassion for the
princess. His whole soul revolted at the dastardly
act. Was not the king growing old? Why, then,
above all others, should he seek to destroy the heir
apparent to the throne? And yet, he must obey the
mandate of the king. Accordingly, he gave the child,
dressed in royal robes, to a herdsman, who lived in the
mountains, and desired him to expose it to the extreme cold, and then return it for a royal funeral. It
is here we can see that no earthly power can frustrate
the will of Heaven. Every prophecy that was foretold by Isaiah and Jeremiah was as sure to come to
pass as the rising and the setting of the sun.

During the absence of the herdsman, his own little
son had been called hence, and when he arrived home
his house was in mourning. Instead of digging a little
grave, he dressed his son in the royal robes taken from

Cyrus, and returned to the palace, where the herdsman had the satisfaction of seeing his son entombed in the sepulchres of the kings. So Cyrus grew up, educated to the hardy life of a mountaineer. The herdsman had educated him in the art of swordsmanship, so that there were none like him in all the country. He was famed for his extraordinary beauty and muscular development. In disposition he was mild and gentle, which drew around him a host of friends. At length, being appointed king in one of their boyish games, he thoroughly scourged the son of a nobleman, and for this act was summoned before King Astyages, and was immediately recognized as the son of Mandane. The king's rage knew no bounds. He immediately transported Cyrus to Persia, and slew the son of Harpagus. In this he made a grand mistake, for as soon as Cyrus had collected an army of Persians around him, a large number of Medes deserted their post and went over to him, on account of the tyranny of Astyages. Harpagus now awaited his opportunity, and as the army of Cyrus advanced he threw open the gates of the city, and Media was overthrown 559 B.C.

His next step was to bring the rich Crœsus, king of the Lydians, under subjection. He knew that Crœsus was learned in all of the arts and sciences, having collected around him the wit of both Europe and Asia. His life, however, was given up to sumptuous extravagance, and he considered himself the happiest man in the world. Proud of his wealth, he arrayed himself in gorgeous clothes, studded with diamonds, and seating himself on the throne gave audience to the wise men of that age. Among them was the learned Solon, one of the seven wise men of Greece, of whom he commanded to know who was the happiest man on earth, believing that Solon would say, Crœsus. Solon's reply was: "A citizen of Athens, who died gloriously fighting for his country." "And who next?" "Cleobis and Biton. Their mother prayed for the best gift Heaven could afford them. Her prayer was immediately answered, for they both fell asleep, and died in a soft and peaceful slumber."

"You do not count me in the number?" said Crœsus. "No. Man's victory is not complete until he gains the crown. No king can be happy during the battle; happiness comes through victory. Hence, the happiest man is he who has passed through the disappointments and sorrows of life, laid down his armor, forded the river, and gained the crown. Moses' greatest victory was on Mount Nebo. Samson's in the temple. Elijah's at the Jordan."

Crœsus was wroth at the answers. Æsop, the hunchback, author of the fables, was at the court on this occasion, and said: "Solon, you must either not come near kings, or else speak that which is agreeable." To which Solon replied: "Say, rather, that we should never come near them, unless we speak for

HILLS AND WALLS OF JERUSALEM.

their good." The death of Atys, his beautiful son, brought Crœsus to a realizing sense that happiness is not contained in riches, and it was in this condition that the hosts of Cyrus found him, and subdued his kingdom, 546 B.C. When Crœsus was condemned to death by Cyrus, and cast on to the pyre, he cried out: "Solon! Solon! Solon!" Cyrus hearing him cry for Solon asked the cause, and on being informed immediately released him, and with his knowledge of science and skillful engineering, coupled with Cyrus, under the power of God, Babylon fell 538 B.C. "Thus saith the Lord to His anointed, to Cyrus: I will break in pieces the gates of brass, and cut in sunder the bars of iron, and I will give thee the treasures of darkness, and hidden riches of secret places, that thou mayest know, that I, the Lord, which call thee by name, art the God of Israel. For Jacob, my servant's sake, and Israel mine elect, I have even called thee by name. I have surnamed thee, though thou hast not known me."

Every man that God called to a place of trust and power was from the loins of Shem. Every kingdom founded by the sons of Ham and Japhet will in due time be overthrown, and the whole world will become "The little stone cut out of the mountain without hands," viz., Israel. It is a marvelous thing that the snare laid for the destruction of Babylon was laid by God himself. "I have laid a snare for thee, who drieth up the waters of the river, who bringeth darkness on

her princes. In their heat I will make their feasts, and
I will make them drunken, that they may rejoice, and
sleep a perpetual sleep, and not awake, saith the
Lord." "I will cut off from Babylon the name. I
will make it a possession for the bittern, and pools of
water. I will sweep it with the besom of destruction,
saith the Lord." "I myself, saith the Lord, will examine with a jealous eye, to see if there be any remains of that city, which was an enemy to my name,
and to Jerusalem." The walls fell down. The Euphrates, no longer finding a free channel, changed its
course; it became a lair for wild beasts, and filled up
with serpents and scorpions, until the site of the city
was lost forever and the prophecies were fulfilled. It
is said of Cyrus that during his entire life he was never
known to utter an angry word. During his reign of
thirty years justice was universally tempered with
mercy, and he admitted that had he allowed Crœsus
to have been burned on the pyre, it would have
blasted the happiness of his entire life. The contrast
between the wars waged by Cyrus and those of other
kings, both sacred and profane, prove conclusively that
he was ordained by God, not only to liberate the captive Jews, but to subdue Asia, and this must be
brought to pass by a humane conqueror. " Thus his
dominions were bounded on the north by the Caspian
and Euxine Seas, on the south by Ethiopia and the
Arabian Sea, on the east by the Indus River, and on

the west by the Ægean Sea. In the midst of this vast empire he resided. Seven months in Babylon, or during the winter season; two months in Ecbatana, during the extreme heat of summer; and three months at Shushan, in Persia, in the fall, where he died." Before closing this chapter, it is well to give the closing scenes of his life, as recorded by Herodotus, which is accepted by some historians and repudiated by others.

" Having a wish that his power should become absolute, and overshadow all Asia, in fulfillment of Astyages' dream, he began an unjust war upon the Scythians, who dwelt on the northeast shore of the Caspian, and after a fierce engagement he retreated, leaving a large quantity of liquors on the field. The Scythians seized the spoils, and when Cyrus returned they had drunken themselves into a profound stupor, which gave Cyrus an easy victory. When the son of Queen Tomrys awoke, and found himself a prisoner among the Persians, he immediately put himself to death. His mother hearing of this sought revenge. and began a second battle with Cyrus. She with her army retreated, as Cyrus had done, drawing them into ambush, and killing two hundred thousand, together with Cyrus. She then ordered the head of Cyrus to be severed from his dead body and thrown into a vat of blood, exclaiming at the same time : ' *Now glut thyself with blood, in which thou hast always delighted, and of which thy thirst has always been insatiable.'* "

This history is not borne out by the facts recorded in the life of Cyrus. That he was mild, gentle, and kind in his disposition, all historians agree, and that he died in his palace, surrounded by the royal household, together with Daniel, there is every reason to believe. Rollin says: "But what decides the point unanswerably in favor of Xenophon is the conformity we find between his narrative and the Holy Scriptures, where we see, that instead of Cyrus having raised the Persian empire upon the ruins of the Medes, as Herodotus relates, those two nations attacked Babylon together. Herodotus' story has more the air of a romance than of a history." Chambers says: "The . . . . work of Xenophon is not a history; it is a historical romance, and was manifestly intended by the author for such. Xenophon wished to picture a great and wise king, and finding the elements both of greatness and wisdom in Cyrus, he took advantage of his historic personality, and engrafted upon it whatever, according to his own notion, would ennoble and dignify it." The reader will now comprehend at a glance just how many difficulties there are attached to a true record of the life of this extraordinary king and conqueror, and can accept whichever accords nearest to their ideas of the truth of either writer. (See Chapter XVI. of this book, entitled "Daniel.")

Darius, according to Josephus, was a son of Astyages, and consequently the brother of Mandane, the mother of Cyrus. Astyages, in the IXth Chapter of Daniel, is called Ahasuerus. It is therefore probable that the moment Cyrus subdued the Median kingdom he gave the sceptre to one of his uncles, as Darius is titular, and not personal, for like the word Pharaoh, it was the name of a number of kings, both of Persian and Median origin. This is shown by the fact that Ahasuerus, the husband of Esther, who is called in profane history Xerxes, was a Persian monarch, and related in no way to Darius the Mede, the son of Ahasuerus. Astyages and Ahasuerus are frequently made one by commentators, as is Zorobabel and Zerubbabel. It will be seen that as soon as Cyrus subdued nations and kingdoms he restored to a large extent, and thus he has been called "generous to a fault."

CHAPTER XV.

BELSHAZZAR.

IN reading the book of Daniel, it would almost appear that the moment Nebuchadnezzar died, Belshazzar ascended the throne, and yet the facts of the case are, that at the death of Nebuchadnezzar Belshazzar was not born. This king began to reign when he was five years old, with his mother as regent; consequently, at the time that the handwriting appeared upon the wall he was twenty-four years of age. Notwithstanding the many prophecies that had been spoken in relation to the taking of Babylon, the entire population considered the city impregnable, from any point, as the river Euphrates ran directly through the city, and there were provisions stored away for twenty years. Hence, when they were encompassed by the Persian army, they, from the walls of the city, laughed them to scorn; and yet the prophecy, "A drought is upon the waters, and they shall be dried up," made no impression upon them. The very river that they relied upon was the cause of their destruction. When the city had been surrounded by troops, they began to throw up earthworks, as in the case of all encompassed cities, so that no thought was taken of this act, as the supposition was that Cyrus knew nothing of the large amount of provisions in store, and that he intended to keep them confined until famine drove them to an unconditional surrender. Deep ditches were dug for miles both above and below the city, so that it was only the work of a few hours to connect them with the river, and thus drain it to the bottom of the channel. There was, however, one thing that stood in the way of victory, and that was the great brazen gates, that closed down over the river every night at sunset. If these were closed, then there would be no need of turning the river. Undismayed, however, Cyrus continued his work of digging the trenches, as if by inspiration. Whether Cyrus at that time knew of the prophecies of Isaiah and Jeremiah is not known, but this we do know, that there was no escape from the fulfillment of the words of the prophets: "Heaven and earth shall pass away, but my word shall not pass away," has been true from the foundation of the world. When the ditches were finished, ready to receive the waters of the river, Cyrus had a dream that an invisible guide would go before him and open the brazen gates that shut down from the quays to the river. The night was at hand. A grand festival was to be celebrated in the city, and all of the lords and ladies, were to be present in the palace, and, as on former occasions, Cyrus knew that the night would be given over to drinking and excesses. The time had come to act. Dividing his army into two companies, the one under Gobrys, at the lower end of the city, and the other under Gadatas, at the upper end, he commanded them to advance. In the meantime the ditches had been opened, and in one hour that part of the river flowing through Babylon was dry. The invisible guide, that promised to go before Cyrus and open the gates, made the keepers subservient to his command, for through the general disorder of preparing for the evening's festivities both gates had been left open. "Thus saith the Lord to His anointed, to Cyrus, whose right hand I have holden, to subdue nations before him, and I will loose the loins of kings, to open before him the two leaved gates, and the gates shall not be shut." "Behold I will punish the king of Babylon in his land, as I have punished the king of Assyria."

Within the city walls all was confusion. The king's palace was thronged from centre to circumference. Thousands were coming in chariots from every quarter of the city, as this was to be the grandest festival of the season. The banquet hall was thronged with thousands of the king's lords and ladies; music sounded from every quarter of the palace, while wine flowed like a river. The revelry had now fairly begun. Belshazzar arose from his throne, and commanded that the gold and silver vessels that Nebuchadnezzar had

pillaged from the temple at Jerusalem be brought
forth and filled to the brim. Then raising a golden
goblet on high, he gave a toast to the gods of gold
and silver. Look! the king turns pale, his countenance
changes, the joints of his loins are loose, his knees
smite one against another. All eyes are now riveted
upon the wall over against the candlesticks. He sees
the fingers of a man's hand slowly but surely advancing. Now he sees a part of the hand, and while he
looks the fingers begin to write. Breathless with excitement, paralyzed with fear, sweating from every
pore, yea, gradually dying, he watches, until the fatal
words are written and the hand vanishes from sight.
Then he cries aloud. The astrologers, the Chaldeans, the
sooth-sayers, quick, give me the interpretation of these
words, and I will make you the third ruler of the kingdom. But, alas! they were too weak. That was the
hand of God, and inspiration alone, through the mind
of Daniel, must fathom it. " Then came all of the
king's wise men, but they could not read it."

At this moment the queen came into the banquet
hall and, seeing the king in trouble, said : " Let not
thy countenance be changed, for there is a man in thy
kingdom in whom is the spirit of the holy gods. He
was made master of the astrologers, in showing hard
sentences and disclosing of doubts. Let him come,
and he will read the handwriting on the wall." Then
was Daniel brought in before the king, to make known

the writing, and was promised to be clothed with scarlet, an emblem of royalty, and have a chain of gold around his neck, an emblem of power, and to be the third ruler in the kingdom. Then Daniel looked up and commenced to read. Slowly and distinctly he pronounced each word. "Mene, Mene, Tekel, Upharsin." God hath numbered thy kingdom, and finished it. "Thou art weighed in the balances, and found wanting." "Thy kingdom is divided, and given to the Medes and Persians."

Notwithstanding that his doom was sealed, his kingdom was ended, his hour was at hand, nevertheless his word had been given, and in the short hour that remained to him on earth he commanded, and Daniel was clothed with scarlet, a chain of gold was placed around his neck, and a proclamation was issued, the last act, and the most honorable act, of the life of Belshazzar, proclaiming him the third ruler in the kingdom. Hark! what means that disturbance in the outer court? The door is thrown open, and Belshazzar stands in the presence of Cyrus. "In that night was Belshazzar, the king of the Chaldeans, slain." "And Babylon shall become heaps; a dwelling-place for dragons." "I will dry up her seas, and make her springs dry." "I will bring them down like lambs to the slaughter." "Then the heaven, and the earth, and all that is therein, shall sing for Babylon, for the spoilers shall come unto her from the north, saith the

Lord." So Jeremiah wrote in a book all the evil that should come upon Babylon, even all the words that are written against Babylon. "And Jeremiah said to Seriah, when thou comest to Babylon, and shall see, and shall read all of these words, then shalt thou say, O Lord, Thou hast spoken against this place, to cut it off, that none shall remain in it, neither man, nor beast, but that it shall remain desolate forever." "And it shall be, that when thou hast made an end of reading this book, that thou shalt bind a stone to it and cast it into the midst of the Euphrates, and thou shalt say: Thus shalt Babylon sink, and shall not rise from the evils that I will bring upon her, and they shall be many." "Thus far are the words of Jeremiah." The prophecies were fulfilled, and Babylon, that mighty city, was lost forever." "Her cities are a desolation, a dry land, and a wilderness, a land wherein no man dwelleth, neither doth any son of man pass thereby."

CHAPTER XVI.

DANIEL.

IN dealing with historical events, we have to take into account the length of time that has elapsed, and the difference of dates existing between various writers. In the succession of kings, from Nebuchadnezzar to Belshazzar, Josephus says: "When Evil Merodach was dead, after a reign of eighteen years, Neglissar, his son, took command, and retained it for forty years. Then came Labosordacus, who reigned nine months, after which Baltsar, under which Babylon was taken, seventeen years." Rollins differs in names, relation, and time, for says that writer: "The reign of Evil Merodach, which lasted only two years, was succeeded by Neglissor, his sister's husband, who was slain in battle in the fourth year of his reign, and was succeeded by his son Laborosarchoid, who reigned nine months, and was put to death. He was succeeded by Belshazzar, who reigned nineteen years." According to the best authenticated computation, we find that Nebuchadnezzar took Jerusalem the first time in the third year of the reign of Jehoakim, king of Judah.

Among the captives were the three Hebrew worthies, together with Daniel, who was twelve years old. From this time is reckoned the time of the beginning of the seventy years' captivity, which was the first year of the reign of Nebuchadnezzar, which lasted forty-three years. At his death, Evil Merodach, his son, was crowned. His reign was one round of debauchery, insomuch that his father's family conspired against him, and slew him two years after his ascension to the throne.

At his death, Neglissor, his brother-in-law, who was the chief conspirator, took the crown and immediately made war with Darius the Mede. Darius sent for his nephew, king Cyrus, and Neglissor was slain, after a reign of three years and three months. Laborosarchoid, his son, then took the crown, but his infamous and barbarous actions incited the people to rebellion, and he was put to death after a reign of nine months. He was succeeded by Belshazzar, who reigned nineteen years. Belshazzar was a son of Evil Merodach, and a grandson of Nebuchadnezzar.

After Belshazzar, Darius reigned two years. Thus Nebuchadnezzar began to reign 606 years B.C.; Babylon fell 538 years B.C., and Cyrus began to reign, after the death of Darius, 536 years B.C., which exactly completed the prophesied captivity. Seven years after Daniel had been carried captive into Babylon, Nebuchadnezzar came again into Jerusalem, and took Jehoa-

kim the king of Judah and a large number of captives,
of whom Ezekiel was one; neither he nor the king
being yet nine years of age. They were taken to
Mesopotamia. These dates will compare very nearly
with those given by Jeremiah lii. 31 : "And it came to
pass in the seven and thirtieth year of the captivity of
Jehoachim, king of Judah, in the twelfth month, in the
five and twentieth day of the month, that Evil Merodach, king of Babylon, in the first year of his reign,
lifted up the head of Jehoachim, king of Judah, and
brought him forth out of prison." The taking of Jerusalem was first under the reign of Jehoakim, 606 years
B.C.; second under the reign of Jehoiachin, 599 years
B.C., and third under the reign of Zedekiah, 588 years
B.C. The captivity of Zedekiah and the death of Belshazzar put an end to both kingdoms. Jehoakim had
reigned three years when Nebuchadnezzar came and
carried Daniel into captivity. He then restored Jehoakim, and he reigned seven years longer in Jerusalem.
In the third year of his second reign Daniel inter-
preted Nebuchadnezzar's dream, and at the age of
fifteen years was made ruler over all Babylon. This
he retained up to the death of Nebuchadnezzar, a
period of forty years. From this time up to the night
of the death of Belshazzar he was the chief book-
keeper, or secretary of state, but on his interpretation
of the handwriting on the wall, he was made third
ruler over Babylon, which he held through the reign

of Darius, a period of two years, when Darius died and Cyrus took the reins of the government.

The prophesied seventy years was now fulfilled, and Daniel took the parchment of Isaiah's prophesies to Cyrus, showing him that the prophet had called him by name nearly two hundred years before he was born, and had prophesied that he would destroy the Assyrian kingdom, liberate the Jews, build Jerusalem, and lay the foundation of the temple, and that if he did not hearken unto the voice of prophecy his kingdom would be wrenched from him and given to another. Having secured from Cyrus a partial promise that he would fulfill the laws and prophets imposed upon him, he remained in Babylon until after the vision of Cyrus, which bore the fruits of restoration, on that same day. He then went away to Shushan, in Persia, where he died eight years afterwards, at the advanced age of ninety years. The only building left standing in that ancient city is the tomb bearing his name.

Ezekiel, after being liberated from Mesopotamia, went to Chebar, where he died while yet a young man among his Jewish companions. Ezekiel began to prophesy when he was nine years of age, continuing for a period of twenty-two years, and dying at the age of thirty-one. During the last two years of the Jewish captivity, Daniel was second to none save the king. During the reign of Darius a plot was formed by the enemies of Daniel for his destruction. The miracle of the three Hebrew worthies did not leave any impression on the king, for he was puffed up with the same pride that characterized Nebuchadnezzar. No charge could be brought against Daniel save that concerning the law of God, and no human power could be brought to bear, that could compel him to deviate one iota from a fixed and immovable trust in Jehovah. He was not surprised then when an edict was thrust before him, decreeing that any one asking a petition of God or man for thirty days, save of the king, should be cast into the lions' den.

As soon as Daniel learned that the king had signed the edict, he being acquainted with the unchangeable laws of the Medes and Persians, went straight to his room, and, opening his window that looked toward Jerusalem, bowed himself down in prayer. This was what his enemies sought, and hence immediately reported it to the king. Now, the king, when he came to himself, was exceedingly sorry, as he now saw through the whole scheme. They would destroy Daniel to elevate themselves, but on account of the law he was compelled to execute it; consequently he called the prophet, and commanded that he be cast into the den of the lions. When Daniel found himself at the bottom of the den, he also found that every lion was surrounded with angels. Like Jeremiah, he was face to face with the angels of the Lord. When the morning came, and the king hastened to the den, he

SINAI.

was surprised to find the prophet ready to bid him good morning. Having been assured that Daniel had rested well, he commanded that his accusers be subjected to the same treatment, and, behold! they were torn to pieces before they had reached the bottom of the den.

Daniel foretold the fourth king after Cyrus, who would attack the Grecians; he foretold Antiochus and his persecutions of the Jews, and the abolition of the sacrifice in the temple; and, finally, the wars of the Alexandrian kings, waged with one another, in Syria and Egypt. Seven years after Daniel removed into Persia, Cyrus died, having reigned in Babylon seven years: nine years from the conquest, and thirty years from the day he became general of the Persian army. As the royal sons, together with Daniel, stood around his bedside, the dying king said: "Enclose my body in neither gold nor silver, nor any other matter, but restore it immediately to earth. I have never seen my soul, but I know that it actually exists, else why are honors paid to the body after death, but if nothing remains of me after death, then fear God, whose power is infinite."

Thus passed away Cyrus, the liberator of the Jews, under the command of the Most High God, the wisest king who ever swayed the sceptre among the eastern empires. It was a fitting tribute to his memory, that Daniel, who was the first captive, and who remained

among them for the full seventy years, should stand
by his open grave and offer up thanks to God for the
gift of Cyrus, the liberator of his people. Daniel lived
one year longer, dying surrounded by the royal household and many of the wise men of the East, as his
fame, like that of Solomon, had extended throughout
all the empires of the world. His entire life was one
of self-sacrifice to the captive Jews and glorification to
the God of Israel. "And they that be wise, shall shine
as the brightness of the firmament, and they that turn
many to righteousness, as the stars forever and ever."

We find, then, in summing up, that there were three
distinguished Jews, viz., Joseph, Daniel, and Mordecai.
Each were second only in the three kingdoms; Memphis, Babylon, and Shushan being the capital cities.
Ahasuerus, the king of Persia, being none other than
Cambyses, the father of Cyrus. It will also be noticed
that as soon as Cyrus subdued nations, he placed upon
the throne one of his own family, and hence, at the
fall of Babylon, the three great armies, viz., the Medes
under command of Darius 1st, the Persians under command of Ahasuerus, and the Lydians under command
of Darius 2d, all joined their forces for the complete
overthrow of the Chaldeans. It will be noticed, further, that at the fall of Babylon the third Darius took
the sceptre, all being sons of Astyages. During the
two years' reign of Darius the 3d in Babylon, Mordecai had succeeded in liberating the Jews in Persia,

who were crushed under the heel of Haman. " For Mordecai the Jew was next unto king Ahasuerus, and great among the Jews." At the death of Ahasuerus and Darius, Cyrus took the crown of both thrones, viz., Chaldean and Persian, and hence the Jews from Babylon under Zerubbabel, and the Jews from Persia under Mordecai, all flocked to Jerusalem to rebuild the city and temple, followed by the blessing of Daniel, one of the most marvelous men recorded in sacred history.

CHAPTER XVII.

THE PROPHETS.

IF two lights are placed in front of the mirror they will produce a double shadow just so long as they are of unequal densities, but the very moment they become equalized they will cast but one. The first is true of all mankind, the last is true of the Redeemer only. Every element within Him was equal, every element of mankind unequal, and thus the peculiar elements in the character of Jonah threw its shadow to us as an eclipse, while God saw the silver lining of the cloud and treated him exactly the same as a benevolent father treats a petulant child.

If we look at the moon when she is waxing from new to full, or waning from full to new, we shall see the shadow gradually removed, from night to night, until she comes forth in all the glory of a full moon without a shadow. She then begins to wane back again until she is lost in shadowy land. If an eclipse of the moon occurs, every eye is turned toward the shrouded satellite and men stand gazing up into heaven, with fear and trembling at this grand phenomena of nature's law, and yet the same shadow that causes the one produces the other. One is just as much a law of nature as the other. On the one we look with supreme indifference, on the other with profound awe. The same is true of the shadow of sleep and death—the one soothes, the other frightens.

In mankind we gauge the reputation, God gauges the character.

Thus with Jonah. To us his acts exceeded his prophecies, and yet, notwithstanding his disobedience, his last act saved a mighty city from destruction.

Jonah was the first of the prophets and flourished under the reign of Jeroboam. Contemporary with Isaiah were Amos, Hosea, Nahum, Micah, and Joel. Contemporary with Jeremiah were Zephaniah, Habakkuk, Daniel, and Ezekiel. Those born in captivity were Zechariah and Haggai. Ezra, a Jewish law-giver, and Nehemiah of the royal house of David, obtained permission to go up and build the temple. They were accompanied by Obadiah and Malachi, the last of the prophets.

Isaiah was poetical and sublime, Jeremiah was heroic and fearless, while Daniel excelled in wisdom and understanding; Joel was the most eloquent, Habakkuk the most vindictive, and Ezekiel the most mysterious; Zephaniah was scholarly, Zechariah pointed, and Haggai earnest; Nahum was classical, Micah was progressive, and Jonah disobedient; Obadiah was brief, while

Malachi observed a sacred regard for all of the laws
written by Moses.

Isaiah's prophecies extend over a period of ninety
years. Beginning at the age of ten years, he prophesied up to the moment of his slaughter by Manasseh.

If his prophecies concerning Cyrus were uttered in
his youth, then there elapsed a peried of two hundred
years between them and his birth, as the death of the
prophet occurred one hundred and ten years prior to
the birth of Cyrus. From this fact his prophecies are
the most marvelous of any contained in the Scriptures,
when brought out separately for investigation.

Speaking of Hezekiah, he says: "Behold the day
cometh when all that is in thine house shall be carried
to Babylon. Nothing shall be left, saith the Lord."
Of the famine in Jerusalem, he says: "For behold the
Lord taketh away from Judah the stay of bread and
the stay of water." In the fall of Babylon he calls
Cyrus by name, and again in the restoration of Judah.
"He is my shepherd and shall perform all my pleasure,
even saying to Jerusalem, thou shalt be built, and to
the temple, thy foundations shall be laid."

Speaking of Jeremiah, he says: "The captive exile
hasteneth that he may be loosed, and that he should
not die in the pit, nor that his bread should fail." In
speaking of Christ: "And the Redeemer shall come to
Zion." Of the dark ages that were to follow the coming of our Lord, beginning in the year 486 A.D., and

ending in 1495 A.D., he says: "For behold the darkness shall cover the earth and gross darkness the people, but the Lord shall rise upon thee." Of the great
highway that has been cut through the desert: " In
that day shall there be a highway out of Egypt to
Assyria, and the Assyrians shall come into Egypt, and
the Egyptians shall serve with the Assyrians."

Historians have thought that if there were any of
the prophecies that could never be fulfilled this would
be the one, and thus we can see that under no circum-
stances can any of the prophecies of God be set at
naught; all must be fulfilled to the letter of the law.

" Therefore the redeemed of the Lord shall return
and come with singing into Zion." " And he said, It
is a light thing that thou shouldst be my servant to
raise up the tribes of Jacob and to restore the preserved of Israel. I will also give them for a light to
the Gentiles, that thou mayest be my salvation unto
the ends of the earth. Arise, shine, for thy light is
come and the glory of the Lord has risen upon thee."
" And the idols he shall utterly abolish."

Nahum prophesied the destruction of Nineveh and
the complete overthrow of the Assyrians; Micah the
destruction of Samaria, the captivity of the Jews, and
their return under Zerubbabel; Joel foretold Christ
and prophesied events that were to take place at Pen-
tecost; Zephaniah prophesied the overthrow of the
Jews, the destruction of the heathen nations, also a

remnant of Judah to be left, which in due time would bless the earth.

Habakkuk prophesied the vengeance of the Almighty against the Chaldeans and thanks God for this just retribution. Ezekiel prophesied the destruction of the Jews by Nebuchadnezzar, the Restoration, and the rebuilding of Jerusalem.

The prophecies of Ezekiel are as mysterious as the Book of Revelations. Those, however, that can be understood have all come to pass.

Daniel was full of wisdom and understanding beyond our knowledge. Like Ezekiel, those prophecies that can be understood were fulfilled. Zechariah prophesied the reuniting of Judah and Israel, the overthrow of Egypt and Assyria, the coming of our Lord in all His glory on Mount Olivet, the millennium, and holiness unto the Lord. "Yea, every pot in Jerusalem and Judah shall be holiness unto the Lord of Hosts." Obadiah prophesied the future glory of the house of Jacob.

Every prophecy, save those that were to come to pass in the fulness of time, have been literally fulfilled.

That they spoke by divine inspiration there can be no reasonable doubt, and that the Bible will be handed down, through all time, as a book of Divine Revelation is a foregone conclusion. If Jerusalem had obeyed the voice of the prophets at the last moment she would have been saved. Nineveh hearkened to the voice of Jonah, and at the eleventh hour escaped destruction.

God is unchangeable towards sin, but changeable in obedience. " For we have not a high priest that cannot be touched with the feelings of our infirmities." " In those days was Hezekiah sick unto death, and Isaiah the prophet, the son of Amoz, came unto him, and said unto him: 'This saith the Lord; set thine house in order, for thou shalt die, and not live.' Then Hezekiah turned his face towards the wall, and prayed unto the Lord, and said: 'Remember now, O Lord, I beseech Thee, how I have walked before Thee in truth, and with a perfect heart, and have done that which was good in Thy sight.' And Hezekiah wept sore. Then came the word of the Lord to Isaiah, saying: 'Go and say to Hezekiah: Thus saith the Lord, the God of David thy father, I have heard thy prayer, I have seen thy tears, behold I will add unto thy days fifteen years.' And God saw their works, that they turned from their evil ways, and God repented of the evil that He had said that He would do unto them, and did it not."

The reader will now take notice, first, the great opposition that existed, in founding kingdoms, up to the hour when Manasseh the great eagle took her flight westward, to found and establish the Kingdom of our God. " And behold, the glory of the God of Israel came by the way of the East," where idols are unknown, slavery overthrown, cities without walls, freedom from the Mosaic law, worship of God, and acceptation of the Branch. As every sun, planet, and satellite are traveling rapidly toward the Pleiades of which Job spoke, so just as sure are all prophecies being rapidly fulfilled. The abolition of slavery was just as surely in fulfillment of prophecy as the restoration of the Jews.

The captive slaves saw the star in the East; they saw Abraham, with an edict in his hand, proclaim liberty to the sons of Ham. The curse of Canaan abolished by the sons of Joseph, light, liberty, salvation, and a glorious resurrection through the Son of God.

CHAPTER XVIII.

MONOTHEISM.

The Hebrews.

" IN that day shall there be an altar to the Lord, in the midst of the land of Egypt, and a pillar at the border thereof to the Lord."

"And it shall be for a sign and for a witness unto the Lord of Hosts in the land of Egypt."

For thousands of years the great pyramid has stood on the borders and in the midst of Egypt, a living miracle of the truth of prophecy.

" Lower Egypt is shaped like an open fan, and the great pyramid is built at the centre or handle, thereby proving from a mathematical standpoint to be not only in the midst but on the border, while Egypt stands in exactly the land centre of the world."

"Around this pyramid were gathered the Hebrew children, their tents occupying the positions of the twelve signs of the zodiac, each tribe knowing the exact position of that sign in the heavens."

" The signet of Reuben, the first born, was Aquarius,

(185)

which means water-pouring, and hence Jacob says of him, " Unstable as water thou shalt not excel."

The signet of Dan was Scorpio, which means conflict, and thus it is written: " Dan shall be a serpent by the way, an adder in the path that biteth the horses' heels, so that his rider shall fall backward."

The signet of Benjamin was Gemini, which means united.

The twelve signs of the heavenly zodiac were given to the twelve tribes in this manner:

" Reuben—Aquarius, meaning water-pouring.

" Simeon—Pisces, meaning fishes, which stand for multitude.

" Levi—Libra, meaning scales, and stands for the law.

" Judah—Leo, meaning lion, which means power, as the Lion of the tribe of Judah.

" Dan—Scorpio, meaning scorpion or conflict.

" Naphtali—Capricornus, a goat, meaning cut off.

" Gad—Aries, a ram, meaning sent forth.

" Asher—Sagittarius, an archer—that is, a destroyer.

" Issacher—Cancer, a crab, meaning strength, to hold fast.

" Zebulun—Virgo, a virgin, meaning purity.

" Joseph—Taurus, a bull, meaning fruitful.

" Benjamin—Gemini, the twins, meaning united."

In this tribal position we can see at a glance the whole plan of salvation as taught from the founding of the Jewish priesthood by Melchizedek (who was none other than the Son of God) up to the moment when he appeared to Nebuchadnezzar in the fiery furnace, with the Hebrew children; still onward to the rending of the veil of the temple; thereby ending the law and establishing the promise.

We begin with the instability of Reuben, as taught in the fall of Adam, to Levi, who were represented with the scales, to typify the law, the service of the temple, and the instruction of the people, up to Judah, who should bring forth the lion of the tribe, to be rejected by them and accepted and united, by the tribe of Benjamin.

Joseph, meaning fruitful, would not only control the granaries of Egypt, but his seed, Ephraim and Manasseh, would control the granaries of the world.

It was in this position, and according to the signs of the zodiac, that the Hebrew children surrounded the great pyramid in the days of Moses, each tribe knowing his position by the position of the stars.

From the Egyptian captivity, up to the days of Rehoboam, they were called Hebrews and also the children of Israel, but from the days of Rehoboam, they took the name of Jews in contradistinction from Israel, hence the term Hebrews, or Israelites, as applied to the Jews of to-day is erroneous, as those terms were used only prior to the time when the twelve tribes were divided into two kingdoms, viz.: The house of Israel and the house of Judah.

The history of this peculiar people begins from the moment God called Abraham up out of Chaldea to establish the true seed of the Lion of the tribe of Judah.

Immediately after Melchizedek, king of Salem, had established the Levitical priesthood, God appeared to Abraham and said unto him : " Know of a surety that thy seed shall be a stranger in a land that is not theirs, and shall serve them, and they shall afflict them four hundred years."

The prophecy was literally fulfilled in the Egyptian captivity.

Again, a promise was given by God Himself, that Sarah should bear a son in her old age, and that she should call his name Isaac, which promise was miraculously fulfilled.

It was not, however, until after Abraham would have offered up Isaac for a burnt sacrifice, that God swore by Himself, saying: " That in blessing I will bless thee, and in multiplying I will multiply thy seed as the stars of heaven and as the sands which are upon the seashore, and thy seed shall possess the gates of his enemies; and in thy seed shall all the nations of the earth be blessed, because thou hast obeyed my voice."

We follow this line of patriarchs up to the days of Jacob, who, on account of a famine in the land entered into Egypt with all of his family, numbering seventy souls. Here they remained four hundred and thirty years. The first thirty years, however, was under the reign of Joseph, but after his death "there arose a king that knew not Joseph."

From this point of time began the four hundred years' captivity, according as God had revealed to Abraham.

Toward the close of the captivity there arose a mighty Hebrew, who had been taught all of the arts and sciences of the Egyptian school. God had been with him from the day he was hid in the ark of bulrushes up to the day he was ordained a prophet and a leader of his people.

The seventy who came into Egypt in the days of Jacob now numbered a mighty nation of three millions of souls.

Day was dawning. The long night of captivity was drawing to a close.

The heart of Pharaoh was growing harder day by day, as one plague after another came upon him, yet God remembered the number of the days of their captivity.

Look! The captives are moving toward the Red Sea. We hear the tramp of that mighty host, and as they pass on we hear another mighty shout. Pharaoh with six hundred chosen chariots, and all the chariots of Egypt, and captains over every one of them, are in hot pursuit.

"Stand still and see the salvation of the Lord, which

He will show you to-day." The rod is raised, the sea divides, the angel of God stands between them and the Egyptians. To the captives it is a pillar of fire; to the Egyptians a cloud as black as night.

"Move on" is the command given by Pharaoh, and they enter into the road of death.

All night long they press onward through the inky blackness into the midst of the sea.

Now we see the Lord of Hosts remove the chariot wheels, then we hear the Egyptians say, "Let us flee from the face of Israel, for the Lord fighteth for them against us."

But alas, it is too late, their hour has come, their sun has set. The arm of Moses is raised, the sea returns to his strength, Israel is saved.

And now their wanderings for forty years, in the wilderness of the Sinaitic peninsula, has actually begun.

The commandments were given to Moses, the Levitical priesthood firmly established, the Passover proclaimed, the Sabbath made holy, and the atonement provided for; but death, that mighty giant, was on their track.

The forty years are past, and we see Moses standing on the top of Mount Pisgah over against Jericho, looking over the promised land from Gilead unto Dan, and we hear the Lord say unto him: "This is the land that I swear unto Abraham, unto Isaac, and unto Jacob, saying I will give it unto thy seed."

"I have caused thee to see it with thine eyes, but thou shalt not go over thither."

Thus it came to pass that out of that mighty host of three million of people, save Caleb and Joshua, none were permitted to enter into the promised land.

The Hebrews had now entered the promised land under Joshua, and continued on as a republic, up to Samuel, the first of the prophets and the last of the judges, when the Hebrew nation became a kingdom under Saul, a Benjaminite; and this form of government continued on up to the death of Solomon, when the kingdom became divided, Judah under Rehoboam the son of Solomon, and Israel under Jeroboam, the Ephraimite.

Here we see for the first time the dividing line between Judah and Israel, and it is from this time that the prophecies concerning them differ in a marvelous degree.

After nineteen kings had reigned over Israel, they were finally conquered by Salmanassar, king of Assyria, and carried away captives 725 B.C.

Twenty kings of the house of David reigned over Judah up to the Babylonish captivity, when Zedekiah was conquered, Jerusalem overthrown, and the temple burned.

After their captivity of seventy years was ended they returned to Jerusalem with the tribe of Benjamin, for the purpose of rebuilding the city and temple for the coming of our Saviour, but at his appearance Judah refused, while Benjamin accepted, as all of his disciples were of the tribe of Benjamin, save Judas Iscariot.

Thus these tribes continued together, up to the year 70 A.D., when Titus besieged Jerusalem.

The commanding general was ordered to batter down the wall, after which they retired to rest, and during this time the Benjaminites made their escape.

When Titus found that this tribe had made their escape, he called his commanding general to an account, and he was speechless.

This, however, was in direct fulfillment of the prophecy of Jeremiah.

The number of Jews killed, as given by Josephus, was one million three hundred and fifty-six thousand four hundred and sixty.

The Jews were then scattered to the four winds of heaven.

"And ye shall leave your name for a curse, unto my chosen: for the Lord God shall slay thee, and call His servant by another name."

The term Israel designates the ten tribes that were lost, while Judah represents the tribes of Judah and Levi, who are to this day living monuments of the throne of David and the Levitical priesthood. The name Israel was given by God Himself, and our Saviour distinctly declares "that he was not sent but unto the 'lost sheep of the house of Israel.'" It is therefore certain that all nations, kindreds, tongues, and people

will be brought to a knowledge of our Lord and Saviour Jesus Christ through the " House of Israel."

> " Evidences above, below,
>   Proclaim the blood they cost;
> And prophecy combines to show
>   ' The Jews were never lost.'

> " Evidence above, below,
>   And all around,
> With prophecy, combines to show
>   ' The Lost Ten Tribes ' are found."

CHAPTER XIX.

LIBERTY TO THE CAPTIVE.

IN a secret chamber leading out of the court of the palace in Babylon, Cyrus, king of Persia, was sitting on a throne, clad in the habiliments of a Knight of the East. The Commandery had been called together for the purpose of freeing the Jews from the Babylonish yoke. The seventy years had expired, and prophecy was fulfilled.

The chamber was in the shape of a parallelogram, thrones being in the East, West, and South, and was fitted up to resemble the lodge-rooms of the temple at Jerusalem.

The tapestry was green and gold. The throne in the East was covered with a mantle of royal purple, while the altar was covered with green, mixed with gold. Over the head of the sovereign master was a triangle bearing the sacred word Jehovah.

An eagle stood on the triangle, with a parchment in his beak, whereon was written in golden letters, "Liberty to the Captives." The jewel worn by the master was a triple triangle bearing the word Shibboleth. His

(194)

loins were girded with a lambskin, or leathern apron, and around his neck was a cable of green and gold. The knights present were of all nationalities. Egyptians, Greeks, Medes, Persians, Chaldeans, and Jews, all sitting side by side, bound together with that strong cord of masonry and brotherly love that will have its full fruition beyond the river. Zechariah the Seer was kneeling before the altar with his head bowed in prayer.

Presently the master arose, and, taking up the parchment, began to read from First Kings. "And his servants said unto him, behold now we have heard that the kings of the house of Israel are merciful kings; let us, I pray thee, put sackcloth on our loins, and ropes over our heads, and go out to the king of Israel. Peradventure he will save thy life. So they girded sackcloth on their loins, and put ropes over their heads, and came to the king of Israel and said: 'Thy servant Benhadad saith, I pray thee let me live, and he said, Is he yet alive? he is my brother.' Now the men did diligently observe whether anything would come from him, and did hastily catch it, and they said, 'Thy brother Benhadad.' Then he said, 'Go ye, bring him.' Then Benhadad came forth to him, and he caused him to come up into the chariot. So he made a covenant with him, and sent him away. This covenant, my brethren, remains binding with us, and will remain among masons till time shall be no longer. Our Grand

Master Hiram Abif laid down his tressle board, faithful to his trust. It remains for us to follow his example through life, exactly in the same manner that he met his death, viz., true to every principle.

"I have long since resolved to liberate the Jews. Their cry has gone up for seventy years, 'Lord, free us us from bondage.' But the time was not yet. Jeremiah foretold the beginning, and the end. He was persecuted, as they have been persecuted, and finally sought a foreign shore, to establish the kingdom of Israel, that will be as enduring as the everlasting hills. Our ark and our pillar are the foundation of a kingdom that can never die. When the last trump shall sound, it will find them at work for the upbuilding of the three grand jewels of masonry, viz., faith, hope, and charity."

But now there comes over me a vision in the night, for I dreamed I was standing in the oracle of King Solomon's Temple, with my eyes fixed on the ark of the covenant, for out of it there arose a halo of glory, in which was a triple triangle, bearing the word Seventy. While I was thinking it should be seven, to commemorate the Sabbath of the Lord our God, I saw standing before the ark of the covenant the king and queen of Israel. Over their head was a diadem, on which was emblazoned, "Judah and Israel." Under their feet was a crown of gold on which was written: "I have established my throne forever."

"I knew then that Judah ruled over Israel, and that when Shiloh came to be led as a lamb to the slaughter, the kingdom would be established, and again, when he came a second time in all of his glory on Mount Olivet, when the angel should swear by Him that liveth forever, that time should be no longer, the throne would still have an heir to meet the coming of our Lord."

If we look at a beautiful sunset, when the day is fast fading into the twilight, and view its rapidly changing colors, or if we look at the rainbow in all of its prismatic glory, while we look behold it dies; and so the beautiful scene vanished from my sight, and in their place stood " Jeremiah the prophet," holding in his right hand an edict, and in his left hand a book containing the prophecies of Isaiah. Over his head was a blazing star on which was written in letters of blood, "Liberty to the captives." Under his feet was written: "Behold I have called thee by name." Breathless I stood while he raised the parchment and read: " Thus saith the Lord, the hour is at hand when all of the laws and the prophets concerning Judah as spoken by Isaiah shall be fulfilled. This day shalt thou proclaim liberty to my people. Shouldst thou not hearken unto my voice, behold I will liken thee unto Samson, through whose death greater acts were achieved than through his life. Obey, and thou shalt live. Disobey, and this night thy soul shalt be required of thee."

As the vision vanished out of my sight I awoke, and seizing a silver trumpet blew a blast that called to my aid the whole household. Dismissing them all but Daniel, I related to him my vision. Daniel replied: "Sound the alarm; call the craft together, and let them go up and build the city and lay the foundation for the temple." Then he fell on his face and wept. The prophecies were fulfilled. For seventy years he had waited for this hour. A youth of twelve years then, an old man of eighty-two now, but he had never wavered in his faith, nor had one murmur escaped his lips.

"I am here to-night to listen to your pleadings for the last time." "Sovereign master." It was Zerubbabel who spoke. "I am here to implore justice and benevolence for my brethren, as I am of the true seed of David. I was born in Babylon a captive slave, and my youth was spent in the brick kilns and under the lash. I have prayed to God as I was nearing my seventieth year to fulfill His promises through Isaiah and Jeremiah. I am the first among my equals, by rank a mason, and by misfortune a captive, and I came to implore that under the Supreme Architect of the universe the king will restore our liberty and allow us to return and rebuild the temple of our God." "Zerubbabel, I have like you, lamented the captivity of your people and I grant your request, and now before the great I AM, set your people at liberty. Return to

your country, rebuild the temple destroyed by my ancestors and its treasures shall be restored. I arm you
with this sword as a mark of superiority over your
equals, knowing you will draw it only in defense of
your God, your brethren, and your family." "I now
create you a 'Knight of the Sword.' May you, 'Sir
Knight of the East,' wear it with honor to yourself,
your country, and your God." Thus saith Cyrus king
of Persia. "All the kingdoms of the earth hath the
Lord God of Heaven given me, and He hath charged
me to build Him a house in Jerusalem, which is in
Judah. Who is there among you of all His people?
The Lord his God be with him and let him go up."

Then there arose Joshua and Nehemiah, and Zerubbabel, and Zorobabel, and Zechariah, and Haggai, and
Ezra, proclaiming, "We will go up." Behold the plum-
met in the hands of Zerubbabel the son of Shealtiel of
the seed royal of the throne of David, the square in the
hands of Nehemiah the governor, the compass in the
hands of Joshua the high priest, while Zorobabel, the
son of Salathiel, whose genealogy had been carefully
traced step by step back to the throne of David, was
given in charge the records which were to become the
Holy Bible, to be read by all of the nations of the
earth, till the mansions of the city of the New Jerusalem were thrown open to all of those who read and
believed.

Thus the true line was carried forward and estab-

lished through the word of God, for out of the loins of
David came Zedekiah, and from Zedekiah, Tea Tephi,
who founded the kingdom of Israel; and from the
loins of David came Zorobabel, and from Zorobabel
the Lord our Righteousness, which is Jesus, who is
called the Christ.

www.ingramcontent.com/pod-product-compliance
Lightning Source LLC
Chambersburg PA
CBHW030834270326
41928CB00007B/1040